THE NEW INTERNATIONAL HOUSE

Whitney Library of Design
An imprint of Watson-Guptill Publications
New York

Author
Francisco Asensio Cerver

Publishing Director
Paco Asensio

Graphic Design
Mireia Casanovas - Albert Pujol

Text
Richard Lewis Rees

Photographers

Water and Glass House **Futjitsuka Mitsumasa.** Zorn House **Korab Hedrich Blessing.** Stainless Stell Apartment **Korab Hedrich Blessing**. Little House **Koji Kobayashi - Nobuaki Nakagawa.** Cube House **Koji Kobayashi.** Circule House **Koji Kobayashi**. House in Sant Jaume Ses Oliveres **Eugeni Pons.** Bom Jesus House **Luis Ferreira Alves.** Amat House **Lluis Casals.** Charlotte House **Behnish & Partner.** Hausler House **Eduard Hueber - Archi Photo, Inc.** Burger House **Eduard Hueber - Archi Photo, Inc.** House in Sakuragoaka **Toshiwaru Kitajima.** Margarida House **Eugeni Pons.** Can Cardenal House **Eugeni Pons.** Dub House **Christian Richters.** Lawson-Westen House **Tom Bonner.**

1997 ©
Francisco Asensio Cerver

Printed in Spain

Published by
Whitney Library of Design
An imprint of Watson-Guptill Publications
New York

ISBN 0-8230-3167-5

Introduction

Ideas cross reality in an oblique way, like steams or currents that constantly double back on themselves, undergoing mutations and successive splittings so that they are slightly transformed by each new displacement.

Creation today is inevitably affected by the speed with which images are broadcast around the world. The profusion of specialist publications in art and architecture converts all formal discoveries into something soon taken for granted on the basis of which many simultaneous variations are produced at different points around the globe. The present expires at the same rapid pace with which these new discoveries are made.

Although each new wave of creation wipes out the traces of its predecessor, fruits of the latter remain scattered over the landscape for many years. The client, the occupant, the purchaser stand behind the architect who, having finished his work, takes his leave and goes elsewhere. Then, at last, they may observe the house alone for the first time, without any form of masking, without interference or justification.

Each work has many different readings, but the most important of all is the aesthetic, although in many cases this is no more than a ghost reading which never becomes reality: a mirage. If we concentrate exclusively on images, it is as though we were looking at ourselves in a mirage, at the face of our own sensitivity. We see our own preferences, nothing else. This is how the gaze works: we manage to retain only what immediately attracts us, which is whimsical and arbitrary. At heart it is merely a crystallization of the images going round in our heads that we recognize when we see them. This is a verification, not a discovery. When browsing through photographs, therefore, for the most part we do not actually see the projects: we simply project our own preferences.

The following reading is far more enriching: if we study the text and pay attention to the plans, we discover the origins of these isolated images. What initially seemed to be arbitrariness or formal fickleness begins to emerge as an interpretation of the site, a response to a specific program or to existing conditions, something that may even reveal a different philosophy of living. We must follow itineraries, stroll through the plans in our imagination, as if we were the true occupants of these rooms, wonder how we would spend the afternoon sitting beside a window or in one of the gardens on the following pages.

The projects featured in *Exclusive Houses* are not picture postcards; they have been selected by virtue of their ability to evoke and suggest emotions. Although they have all been built in recent years, what is outstanding about them is not so much their novelty as their spatial qualities and the way they interpret the landscape. Despite the fact that the themes are almost invariably the same (they are, after all, eternal) —light, approaches, perspectives, the expressiveness of materials— the solutions are different in each case. The formal purity of Shirakawa's houses contrasts with the overlapping geometry and distinct structures of the Lawson-Westen House by Eric Owen Moss. The bright, polished surfaces of Krueck & Sexton's Zorn House constitute the reverse counterpart to the architecture of Günter Behnisch's home. The hermetic, jewel-like aspect of the Can Cardenal guest pavilion complements the warm-colored walls, the pergolas and terraces of the Amat House. Kengo Kuma works with transparent materials: glass and water; Eduardo Souto de Moura with the rough, wrinkled texture of undressed stone against the purity of completely whitewashed wall facings. Bolles and Wilson use colored planes and different materials that overlap each other.

It would be difficult for anyone traveling to Japan, California, Portugal, Illinois or Germany to visit all these houses. And even if they could, it would be practically impossible to visit their interiors: they are all private homes. Nevertheless, a phenomenological approach to each project is possible, for although the articles reflect the demands of clients and the work of architects, for you the reader each image and each text constitute a snippet of reality that will allow you to reconstruct the houses in your mind, just as they were conceived, and subsequently make them your own for your own enjoyment.

Water and Glass House

The materials are always light:
glass, steel or wood.
These, Kuma says, are materials of the present.

Kengo Kuma

Born in Kanagwa (Japan) in 1954, Kuma graduated in architecture from the University of Tokyo in 1979. In 1985-1986 he held a scholarship from the Asiatic Cultural Council as guest student at the University of Columbia. In 1987, while lector at the University of Hosei, he set up the Spatial Design Studio. Kengo Kuma & Associates was founded in 1990.

The Water and Glass House was designed mainly for guest accommodation. The square footage is 3,694 in three floors and the building occupies half of the site's 4,206 square feet on the edge of the Atami clifftops, overlooking the Pacific Ocean.

Although in recent years Japanese architecture has made frequent use of concrete as a construction material, Kuma considers it too heavy and excessively monumental. As an alternative, therefore, the architect adopted the principle of transparency, building his houses from "meatless" materials through which it is possible to see.

By virtue of their lightness, glass, steel or wood are used. These, Kuma says, are materials of the present. Furthermore, the structure becomes lighter as it increases in height.

The top-level floor lies under a 6-inch-deep sheet of water which reflects one oval and two square glass volumes sheltered beneath a metal slat roof. For Kuma this house does not really have a roof, nor does it have walls: only the minimum number needed for security reasons. Wherever possible he used glass as the building material, while the walls have lost density and become transformed into filters. The architect wanted people on this floor to feel as if they were floating on water.

The Water and Glass House is entered from the garage through an open door in a granite wall, which leads directly out onto a concrete and steel bridge spanning a stretch of water on the floor below. The different dependencies are arranged around this open vertical reception space where the stair is situated. The ground floor accommodates a Japanese-style room, an administration room, a meeting room and a gymnasium. The dining room is on the access-level floor, oppo-→

The top-floor dining room,
over the sheet of water, is
a transparent, oval volume.

Ground floor
1: sheet of water,
2: Japanese-style room,
3: administration room,
4: meeting room,
5: boiler room,
6: dressing room,
7: sauna, 8: bathroom.

Second floor
10: dining room,
11: entry,
12: open space,
13: kitchen,
14: sushi bar,
15: bridge, 16: garage.

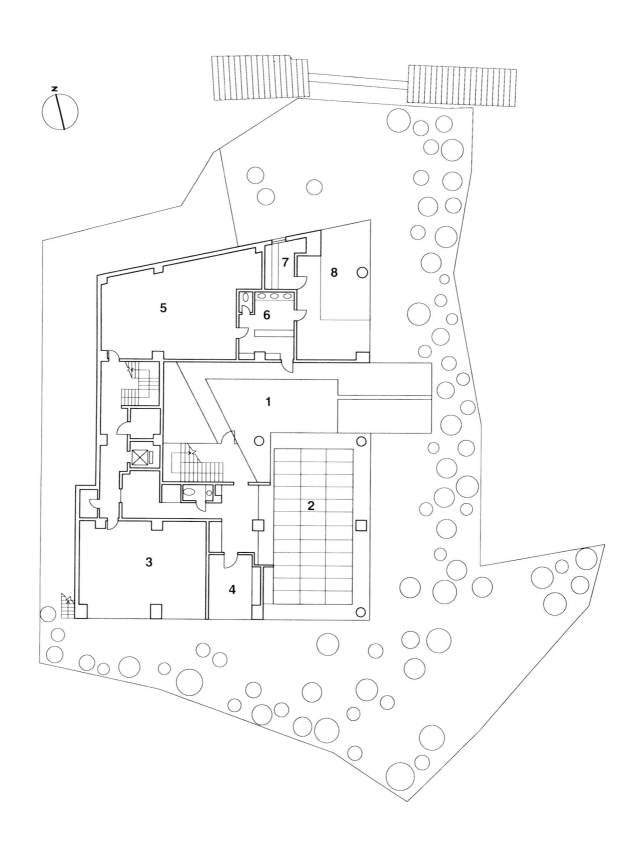

site the door and oriented toward the south, with the kitchen and sushi bar on the right and the guest rooms on the left. The two rectangular top-floor volumes contain guest rooms, while the dining room is in the oval volume.

The house originated partially as a critique of pre-defined forms that have become trite, conventional notions of what a villa should be. Above all, though, it constitutes a reflection on the act of seeing and being seen. In an essay by Kuma titled "To See and Be Seen", he rejects the idea of architecture conceived as a representative or monumental object linked in broad terms to the idea of the Panopticon, an object visible from any point and, at the same time, from which it is possible to see everything. This kind of spatial structuring, observable in many different forms of architecture, is a main target of criticism on Kuma's part, for whom the only way possible to mediate between subject and object when they are forced to confront each other is to eliminate that keen watchfulness characteristic of the →

The Japanese-style room.

The light, translucent stair with glass steps and a metallic structure.

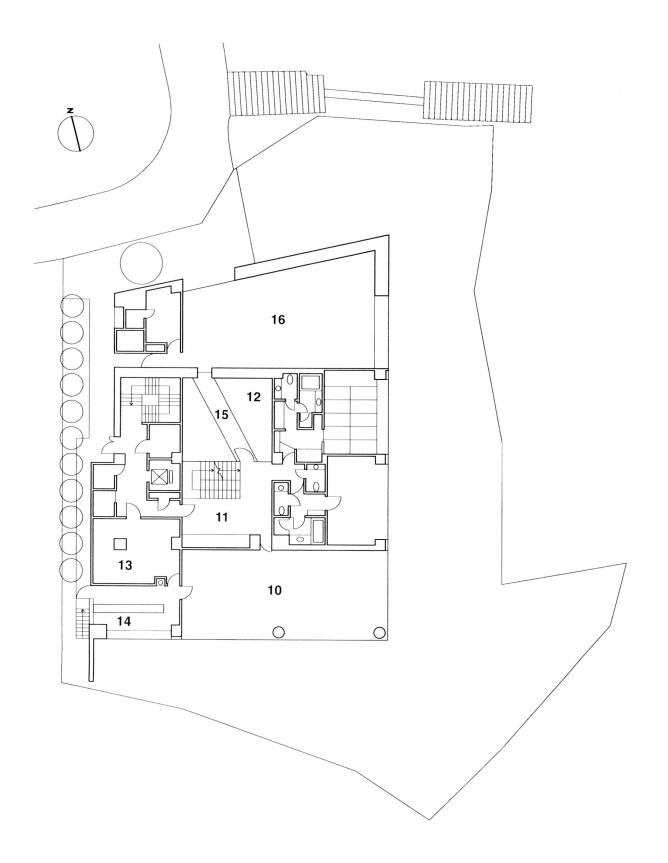

The space spanned by the bridge as it enters the house receives natural light from above.

Panopticon layout. An analysis of different ways of seeing nature, in this case, constitutes the central theme of the Water and Glass House, in which a series of filters and frames stands between the house and the subject. It is possible to see through these, and in this way the materials reveal their transparency. In lieu therefore of the watchful object, translucent layers duplicate images and configure the intermediate space between nature and the subject.

Kengo Kuma's architecture experiments with possibilities of penetrating the very act of seeing, which is neither watchfulness nor control but an intermediary between subject and exterior space. The house is defined not as an object but as a diversity of spaces resulting from the superimposition of different transparencies transfixed by the landscape. Elements such as the sheet of water on the top level, which melds with the sea beyond, or the metal-slatted roof that tones down the light, are treated as filters or abstract frames rather than as obstacles.

An overall feeling of calm and balance and the objective use of materials inform the whole project, which reveals a clear kinship with representative works of the Modern Movement such as Mies van der Rohe's Farnsworth House. This by virtue on the one hand of the dematerialization process the architecture undergoes and, on the other, of the precise, objective, technological use of architectural elements and their unions. Take, for example, the impeccable way in which one pane of glass is joined to the next. In a different sense, the flowing quality of the interior spaces also reflects this affinity.

Kuma believes that the life which unfolds in buildings is more important than the form of their architecture; consistent with this idea, he designs inner circulation routes to arouse the maximum possible interest.

On the other hand, this house has its sources in nature or the landscape, which shares in the life which unfolds here. Indeed, nature acquires meaning when it enters into a relationship with →

Reflections in the glass
surfaces multiply
images.

The slatted roof over the
top floor.

Top floor
9: guest bedroom,
10: dining room,
11: entry,
12: open space.

Section.

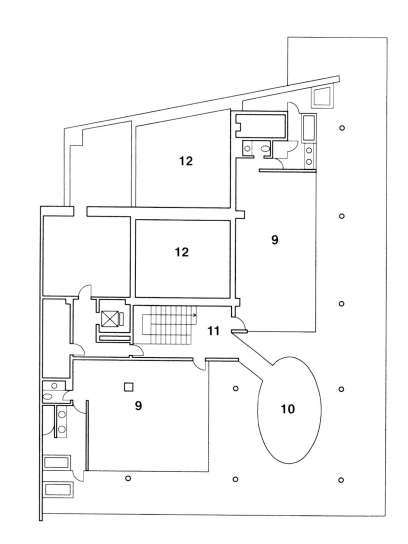

the architecture, which provides it with a frame. Thus, the architecture establishes an open-ended relationship with the exterior: there is no clear differentiation between inside and outside. Far from being introverted, Kuma's spaces share the exterior. The Water and Glass House is therefore understood as a succession of translucent skins whose purpose is to produce effects of transparency, continuity, and, in some cases, shadow.

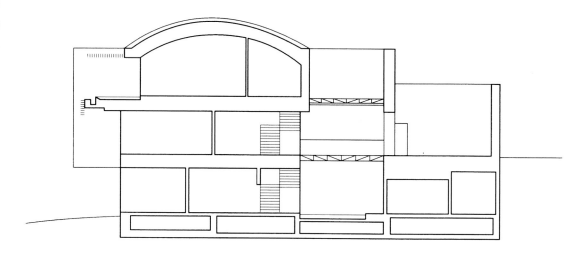

The glass volumes and the pillars seem to float on the water.

In order to understand the architecture of Kengo Kuma, one need only contemplate these views of the sunrise and the night from the Water and Glass House.

Zorn House

The nakedness of an essential language
on the one hand and multiple forms providing greater freedom of
spatial organisation on the other.

Krueck and Sexton architects

Ronald A. Krueck studied at the Architecture Department of the Illinois Institute of Technology (1970), where he now teaches. After collaborating with C. F. Murphy Associates and Hammond Beeby Associates, he founded the firm of Krueck & Olsen (1978-1991). Marck P. Sexton also studied (1980) and teaches at the I.T.T. Having worked with Skidmore Owings & Merrill and Danforth Rockwell Carow, he joined Krueck & Olsen (1980-1991), which became Krueck & Sexton in 1991.

Krueck and Sexton's architecture echoes an old, two-sided controversy, rekindled some years ago in the Berlin Kulturforum area. On one side, the Mies van der Rohe Neue Nationalgalerie, and opposite, the Hans Scharoun Philharmonic: two aspects of modernism which have never really ceased to regard each other with mistrust. The constituent elements of this dichotomy are naked, essential language on the one hand and

greater freedom of spatial organisation, with a multiplicity of forms, fragments and organic developments in search of specificity on the other.

Mies' geometric abstractions, within the context of so-called New Objectivity (Neue Sachlichkeit), constitute Krueck and Sexton's working material, which might be interpreted as a critique of Expressionism, a concept generally used to →

Access is not frontal; a brick wall privatizes the entry.

View from the street.

Superposition of elements and materials: brick, marble, the long window, and the metal pieces painted in primary colors.

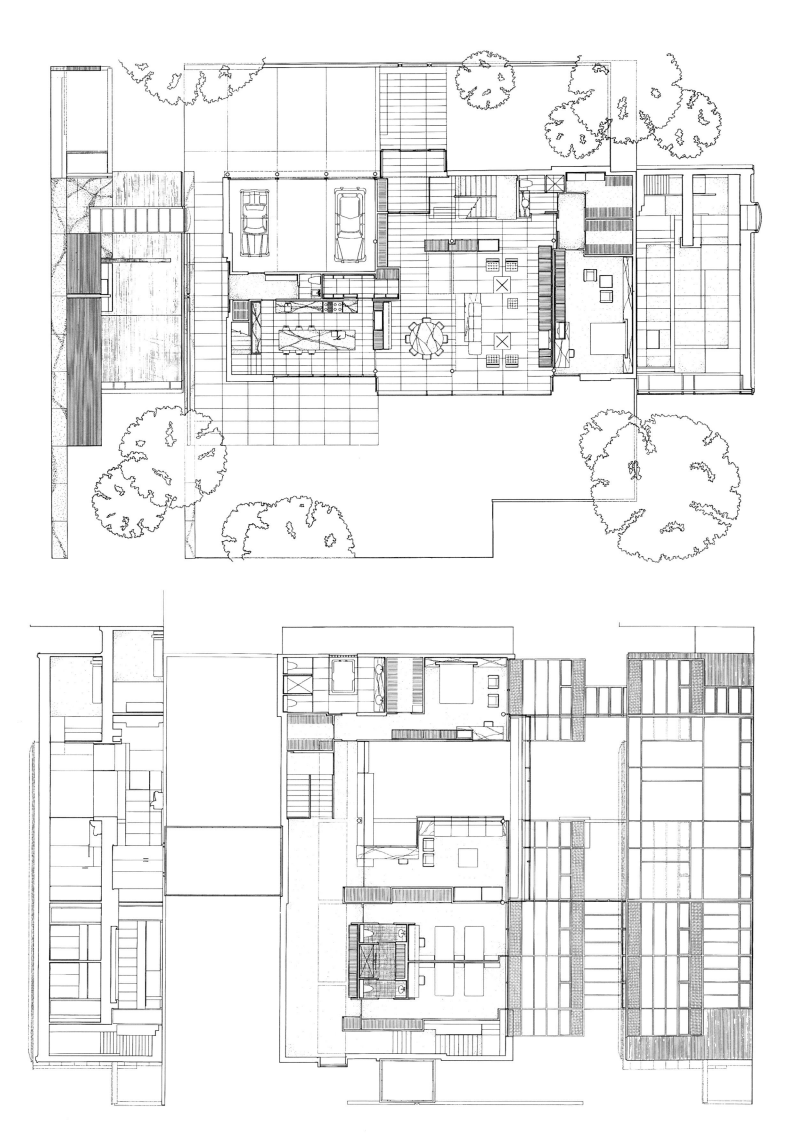

The ground floor and cross sections.

The upper floor and longitudinal sections.

The house front recalls compositions by Mondrian.

describe architecture close to Scharoun's. The architectural trend toward objectivity seems to have been invariably opposed to the idea of Expressionism, in that it is informed by an abstract language of straight lines and right angles thoroughly lacking in organicist elements; by visible metallic structures and large glazed or smooth, polished, lacquered surfaces. Details and materials, exclusively industrial products, are the tools Krueck and Sexton use to identify the distinct elements.

Although this style of architecture is far removed from the idea of context as support for the project, neither does it denote a quest for absolutes. On the contrary, it examines possibilities as the means to generate spaces and allow projects to develop.

Each building or space is an explicitly independent work that responds to the functional demands of the client, considered as the catalyst that activates the project on the basis of the work premises behind this research into modernism. This bond between the client's needs and constant experimentation with a specific pre-→

The south facade is a surface rich in transparencies.

View from the central space.

defined language leads, in turn, to new or unexpected solutions. Elements are often either stretched or compressed in response to tensions, or in some cases curved due to the effect of unbalanced forces.

"Less is More" said Mies, alluding to the rich contents of exercises in purity that eliminate waste and are ever-sparing with images. Clarity and simplicity are more than excess and debauchery. Nonetheless, Krueck & Sexton's relationship with the architecture of Mies is not only ideological: it is no coincidence that one of their projects, The Stainless Steel Apartment (Chicago, 1992), a split-level home for a young family, is located on the top floors of one of Mies van der Rohe's steel and glass apartment blocks.

The Zorn House, set in a north-Chicago residential suburb, is laid out on the site in such a way as to break the rhythm of the adjacent facades and take advantage of the views toward the south. The owners, a couple with two children, were unhappy with the narrow rooms and inadequate natural lighting in their former home.

The house was designed as a simple brick and glass volume whose interior articulates around a double-height communal space.

The south facade is the most transparent, responding to the need to admit as much light as possible. A long, narrow, vertical window overlooking the street opens to the west, jutting out slightly from the facade. At the same time it stretches up to the roof, providing overhead light which evenly floods the central part of the second floor.

The departure point of Krueck & Sexton's architecture is the concept of the rectangle. Originally conceived as a pure rectangle, the house has

been modified: the rectangle has been slightly broken, has undergone slippage and different fragments have been superimposed. The fractures and displacements are produced sometimes in section and sometimes in plan. In this way the different volumes maintain their individuality while forming part of a unitary composition. Though complex, the spaces resulting from these operations are combined in such a way as to create a sense of balance.

As in all of Krueck & Sexton's projects, each part or situation re-affirms the global conception: starting from an intuitive first approximation and after many transformations, a harmony is achieved which reintegrates the previously fractured elements. The design process then ceases to be subjective and the objectivity of the project is attained at the moment when each part takes up its position within the whole.

Previous page:
Detail of the interior.

This page:
Perfection of detail and
the free use of colors
characterize the interior.

Following pages:
The dwelling is
arranged around the
double-height central
space.

Three steps indicate the
position of the stair.

Stainless Steel Apartment

Refurbishment of one of Mies van der Rohe's and modern architecture's **most paradigmatic buildings,** *conducted almost 50 years later by his very successors at the I.T.T.*

Krueck and Sexton architects

Krueck & Sexton's project consists of the refurbishment of a duplex on floors 25 and 26 of the famous Mies-designed block at 860, Lake Shore Drive, Chicago. The apartment is oriented to the south and east, with splendid views over Lake Michigan (to the east) and downtown Chicago.

As students and later as teachers at the Illinois Institute of Chicago, Ronald A. Krueck and Marck P. Sexton can be considered the heirs to the architectural vision and theoretical teachings of Mies van der Rohe. In this sense, it is of enormous interest to see the results of the refurbishment of one of Mies' and modern architecture's most paradigmatic buildings, conducted almost 50 years later by his very successors at the I.T.T. Moreover, not only the architects but also the clients wanted the apartment design to constitute an extension of the architectural concept of the building. The apartment is for a young couple with two small children. The more informal communal spaces are on floor 25: the kitchen, the dining room, a small study and a living room, together with the children's rooms, two lavatories and the laundry room. The floor above accommodates the master bedroom, with a large adjoining bathroom and wardrobe as well as a larger living room and a smaller interior office, lit by a translucent glass pane from the stair that links both floors. →

Detail of the entry and the stair.

General view of the dining room and the study on the lower floor, with a view of the city in the background. The stainless steel cupboard divides the two spaces, which nevertheless share the same table.

All the communal areas are arranged around a single space although they are visually separated, at least partially, either by furniture or by the stair set right in the middle of the room. These elements overlap each other or else they are transformed, introducing constant paradoxes into the apparent conceptual simplicity of the house. Thus the dining-room table and the one in the small lower-floor study are the same piece, and though from the kitchen it is seen as a continuous element, it is in fact divided by a stainless steel cupboard. This cupboard, in turn, rests upon a low counter with a granite top, superimposed on the wooden platform that supports the steel stair. The spaces are related through transparencies and reflections on the bright stainless-steel, granite and glazed terrazzo surfaces. The small lavatory next to the living room is separated from this by a translucent etched glass pane; between the kitchen and the dining room, coinciding with the steps, Krueck and Sexton have arranged some vertical sheets of the same type of glass. The cupboards are perfectly hermetic volumes of stainless or lacquered steel, some slightly displaced with respect to others like in ➝

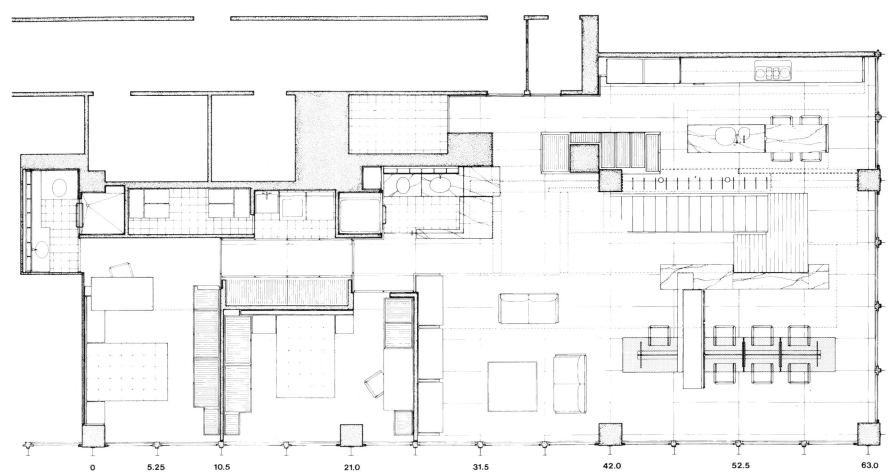

0   5.25   10.5   21.0   31.5   42.0   52.5   63.0

A view of the small living room on the lower floor. The gray tones of terrazzo, of the granite surfaces and of the steel sheets abound throughout the apartment.

Lower floor plan.

Plan of the upper floor.

Detail of the kitchen. The stair acts as a visual sieve between space and dining room.

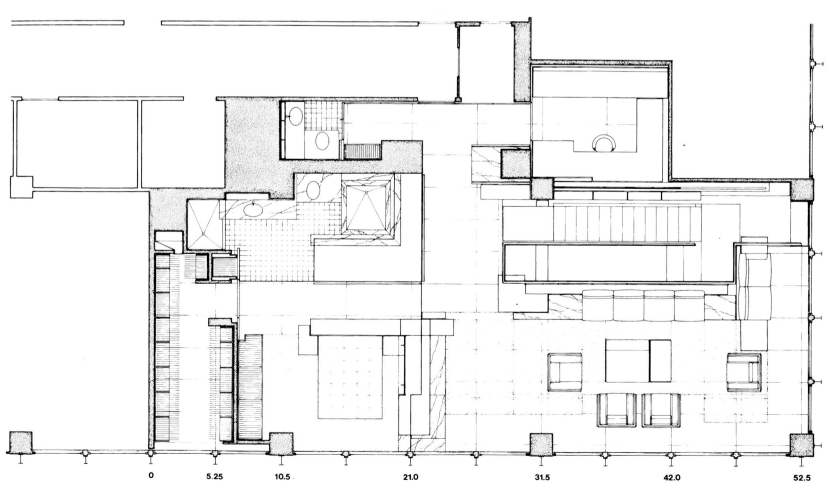

| 0 | 5.25 | 10.5 | 21.0 | 31.5 | 42.0 | 52.5 |

a cubist composition or neoplastic sculpture. Study of the lighting led the team of architects to carefully design the false plaster ceiling. The different levels allow the necessary lights to be concealed in sections and offsets and, by virtue of this, a considerable amount of the light in the apartment is indirect.

As in many projects by Mies, Krueck & Sexton use cupboards as separators between the more private areas and the communal spaces. This project mechanism is perhaps most clearly seen on the floor above, where an L-shaped cupboard separates the living room from the master bedroom. The cupboard does not reach all the way to the ceiling, and a pane of glass has been fitted into the small gap remaining to prevent noise transmission. For the same reason, the passages feature transparent glass swing doors, lacking even handles, to preserve visual continuity. Even so, the continuity of space is partially lost: in such small spaces, continuity and isolation have proven to be irreconcilable.

The apartment presents a generally homogeneous image, the same type of materials hav- →

General view of the stair, made of stainless steel steps anchored to a single side beam cantilevered on the opposite side.

Detail of the foot of the stair, where the wooden surface overlaps with the long granite counter.

Detail of the upper floor balcony, with views over Lake Michigan. The refurbishment of the apartment was required to adapt to the building's exterior carpentry.

The handrail consists of several layers of overlapping, lacquered, stainless steel.

View of the top-floor landing.

General view of the upper floor living room. Much of the furniture was designed by the architects themselves.

ing been used throughout: glass, steel and polished stone. The profiles of all the elements are strictly geometrical. White predominates, tempered by the metallic grays and violet gray of the granite, with the occasional exception such as a red-lacquered tube near the stair or the varnished wooden doors of some of the cupboards. In a way, the interior aesthetic echoes the all-pervading sight visible from inside: that of downtown Chicago, of the steel and glass skyscrapers, of the perfectly geometric profiles, of the burnished, reflecting facades, of blue-grays with small red inserts, neon signs or emergency lights.

The armchairs and the sofas are the same color as the finishes.

The passage door is almost invisible.

Detail of an opening around the bathroom in the floor-ceiling assembly that connects both levels. In the background, the translucent glass pane which admits light into the office.

Little House, Cube House and Circle House

Naoyuki Shirakawa
Three ideas on the same concept:
the little house, the cube house and the circle house

Naoyuki Shirakawa

Born in Kitakyushu (Japan), Naoyuki Shirakawa studied architecture at the University of Kyoto. From 1974 to 1987 he worked for Ishimoto Architects and Associates until, that latter year, he set up his own studio in Tokyo.

Shirakawa's architecture is based on geometrical principles and pure volumes as the generating principle and working tools of his well-balanced projects. He frequently uses simple figures such as the cube and the sphere, submitting them to transformations until they acquire a certain degree of spatial complexity.

His architecture develops its own internal order through the use of imposing objects that transmit a sensation of calm. His houses contain inner paths and oases of tranquillity whose quality varies according to the different types of light they receive. There is no uniformity of spaces in Shirakawa's buildings: variation, the contrast between opposites such as dark and light, full and empty, active and passive, dry and wet, closed and open, creates a surprise-generating polarity. This polarity, ever changing to meet the demands of different situations, forms the core of each project. The point of surprise, that is, the point of maximum interest, is found in the separation between the qualities of one place and those of another. It might be said that this tension shapes the project, a tension which is furthermore the product of experience, engendering contrasts which can be appreciated as one moves through these spaces and observes the transition from one to another. This is the moment when it is possible to really experience Shirakawa's architecture.

In keeping with the Japanese architectural tradition, some spaces look for transparency and a flexible, fluid mutual relationship, achieved through the use as separators of thin, mobile, occasionally translucent partitions. The spaces open onto the private patios his houses normally feature, admitting light either from these patios or else directly from the exterior when an open relationship between the dwelling and its surroundings is possible. On the other hand, Shirakawa's projects echo neither the disorder nor the bustle of their site; on the contrary, they seek the path to tranquillity in what might be a noisy environment. In some cases, indeed, recognition of the potential hostility of the context constitutes the starting point for his projects, leading to closed buildings that shun a frank relationship with the exterior; they might be considered, rather, as a reaction to the disorder of this context.

Three ideas, one concept.
Little house (1996),
Fukuoka, Japan.

Cube house (1992),
Tokyo.

Circle house (1996),
Fukuoka.

Little House

Ease of movement had to be guaranteed,
especially *the feasibility of walking*
from one room to another.

The city of Kitakyushu, like Kobe to the east, is set in an area between the coast and the mountains. Toward the west it becomes a stretch of railway lines, a characteristic highly appropriate to the city's function as gateway to the island of Kiushu to the south. An industrial area lies nearby, bounded on one side by the coast. Thanks to the mountain chain aligned to the east, this part of Kitakyushu is a tranquil spot with a pleasant, varied landscape, in contrast to the city's western zone.

With the rise in land prices during the eighties, the residential areas underwent a major transformation, giving way to a series of larger buildings complete with garages standing side-by-side. The 644 square-foot site on which this project stands is located in one of these zones, immersed in frantic urban bustle. The built area of the plot is 319 square feet and the dwelling's total square footage is 365. Because of its situation, the ground floor is closed on all four sides, while the second floor opens out to the east and west.

There are two essential features of this house: the section, which determines the elevations, in turn drawn as if they were the section, and the handrails running throughout the whole building. Consideration had to be given to the physical health of the clients, an old couple: the husband had been hospitalized some time before and his wife had begun to feel the effects of old age. Ease of movement thus had to be guaranteed, especially the feasibility of walking from one room to another in the event that one member of the couple were to become physically incapacitated in the future. This is the reason why a →

Detail of the east facade.

East facade.

South facade.

Views of the south-east zone.

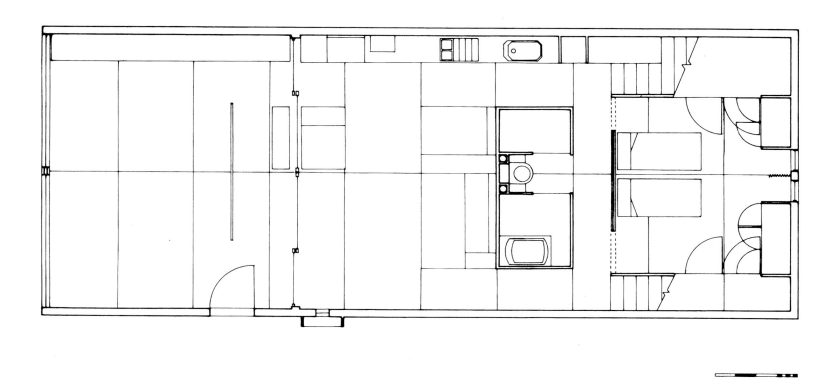

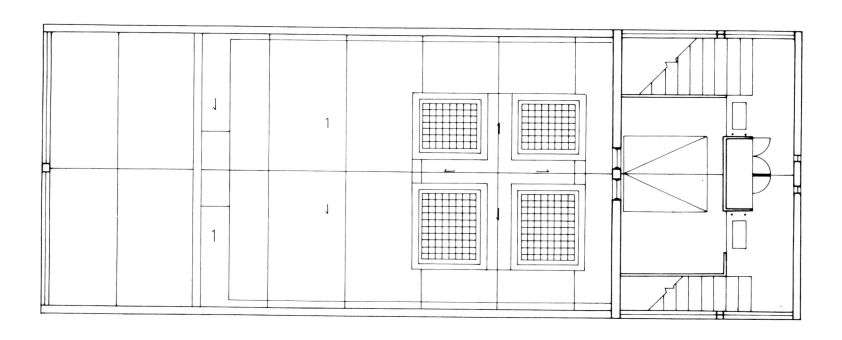

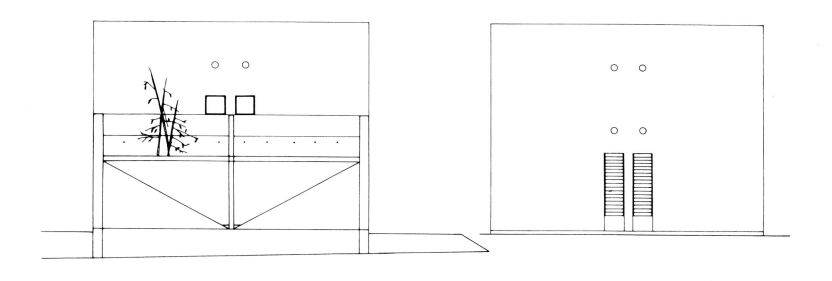

series of painted tubular steel handrails link each room with the next.

The entry, in the east wall of the house, provides access to a reasonably large patio occupying the south part and endowing the dwelling with privacy. From this patio access is gained to the interior through the glass doors which lead to the garden.

The areas and installations which require water, such as the kitchen sink, the bathroom and lavatory, are arranged in the center of the dwelling.

The bathroom and lavatory together constitute an independent freestanding block around which it is possible to walk without having to open any doors.

Thanks to the simple layout of the house, its northern part is a peaceful haven where the bedrooms have been placed, while the south is the area of most activity in that it contains the living and dining rooms.

Both architect and clients agreed that the bedrooms would have to offer varying degrees of →

The living room, dining room and kitchen.

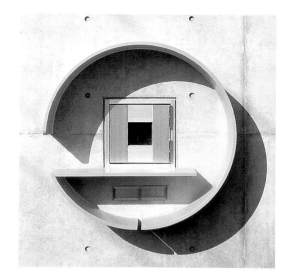

Detail of the letter box.

The entry.

stimulus should the occupants be confined there during long spells of illness or convalescence. An effort was therefore made to install a large number of accessories which would provide such stimulus. To this end, for example, the possibility was considered of moving one of the beds to the south part, where there is more movement.

Two areas, which run along the whole of the long wall, are designed to function as kitchen counters and places to hang clothes. Those who are either cooking or doing the washing are therefore always in full view and, at the same time, can see people walking in the garden. The hall has been eliminated. The letter box has been designed so that the mail arrives directly inside and, just above it, a small window makes it possible to identify callers. All these details are designed to make daily life easier for the old couple. To facilitate maintenance, the tubing and electrical installations are uncovered and are hidden behind the sofa in the living room and behind the table in the dining room. The third floor has been conceived in such a way that if the old couple require constant care and attention, their relatives can live with them. In this case, the children will be able to keep an eye on their parents simply by looking through the staircase skylight.

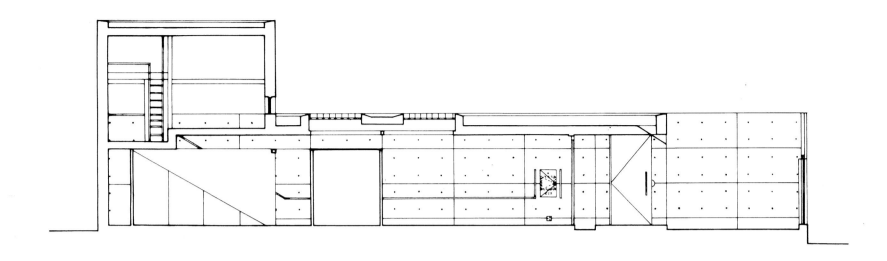

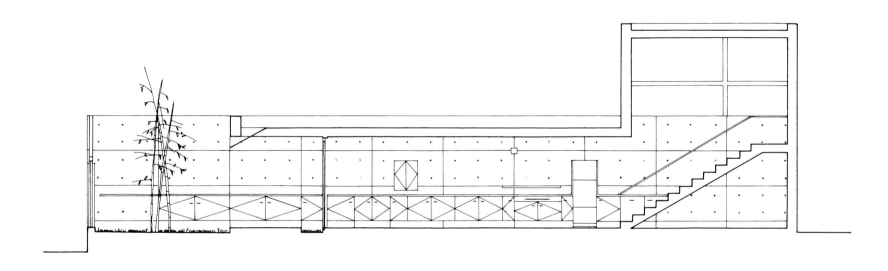

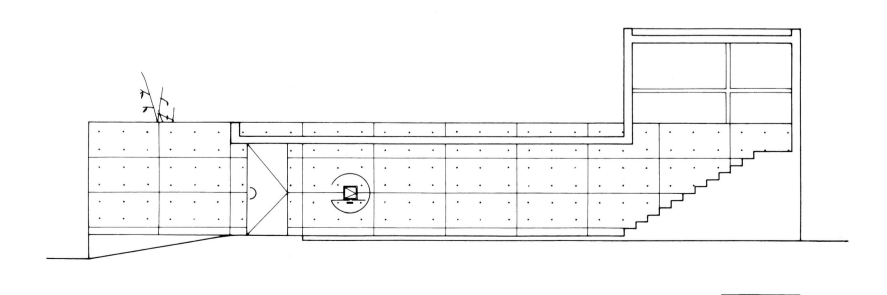

Longitudinal sections.

East elevation.

West elevation.

Detail of the stair.

On the ground floor
looking east.

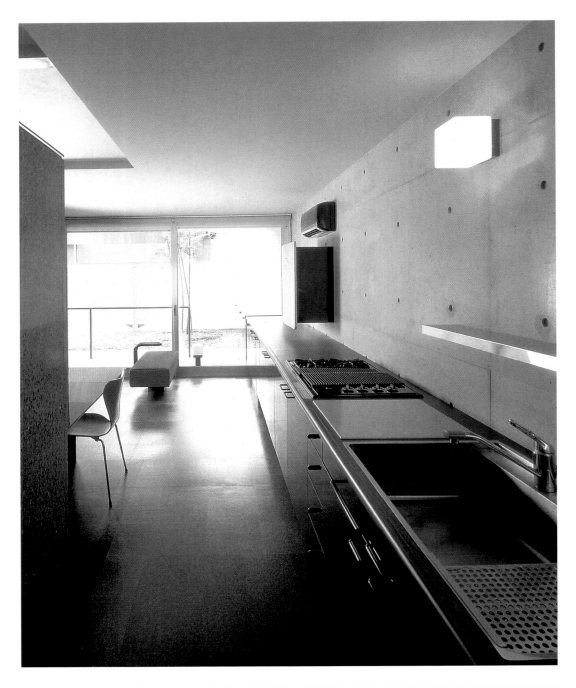

The kitchen.

The bedroom in the north zone.

The dining room.

The Cube House

The elements, openings or stairs
are treated as abstract forms,
with which it is possible to make compositions.

This house, a 20 x 20 x 20 foot cube, stands in the centre of Tokyo on a narrow 230 square-foot site. As the clients have no children they did not need a big home, so its total square footage amounts to only 194.

The bare concrete square which forms the south facade has been split by a joint into four equal square parts into which a circumference has been cut and an intense red-colored strip superimposed. The strip climbs diagonally from the left, where there are a few steps and the small door separating the site from the street. The low wall of large horizontally-placed stones acts as a baseboard on which a row of bushes has been planted. To the right, a tree disguises the sharp edge of the facade, a simple composition of abstract shapes on a square base, fruit of the architect's experiments with both form and materials.

Geometry provides the basis of the project. The position of each element has its origins in the parameters or processes of geometric analysis. The circumference of the entrance facade is exactly determined to be tangential to the →

South facade.

View of the patio from the roof.

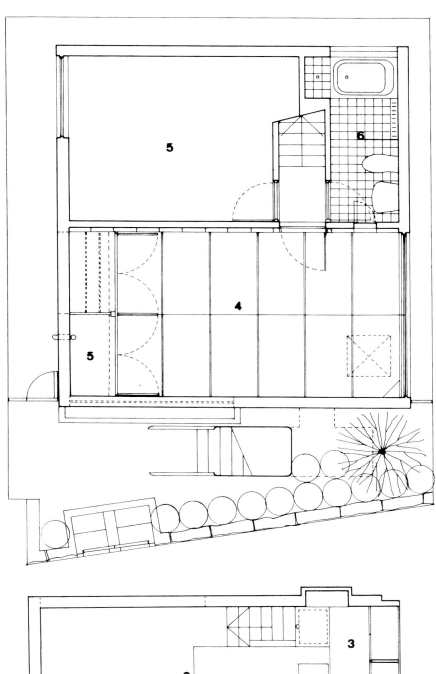

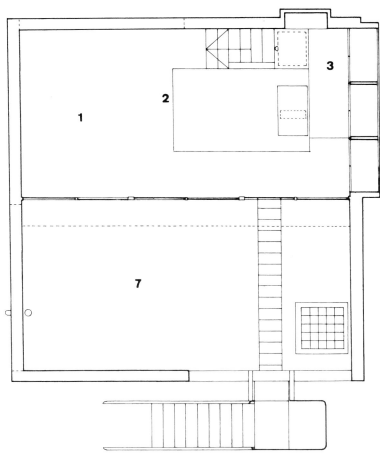

joints which lay down the pattern for the facade plan. This circular hole is the entry to the second-floor patio, which opens into the living room. From the street, through this figure cut out in the wall, one can sense what lies behind: part of the house can be seen and, above it, the sky. The red-painted metallic parallelogram contains the stair. The elements, openings or stairs are treated as abstract forms with which it is possible to make a composition based on laws that go beyond the conventional use of project elements: in the living room, for example, the table is a large plane overhanging the stair, under which you have to pass on climbing up to the second floor. At the circular aperture a long, narrow rectangle, resembling a path to be used by one person at a time, crosses the patio on a bed of jet-black stones that contrast with the red of the exterior stair. To the right of this path, a square of translucent bricks constitutes the skylight over the tatami room on the floor below. A little further on, four concrete stools shaped like inverted pyramids have been sunk into the ground next to the wall. These elements make up the patio, which

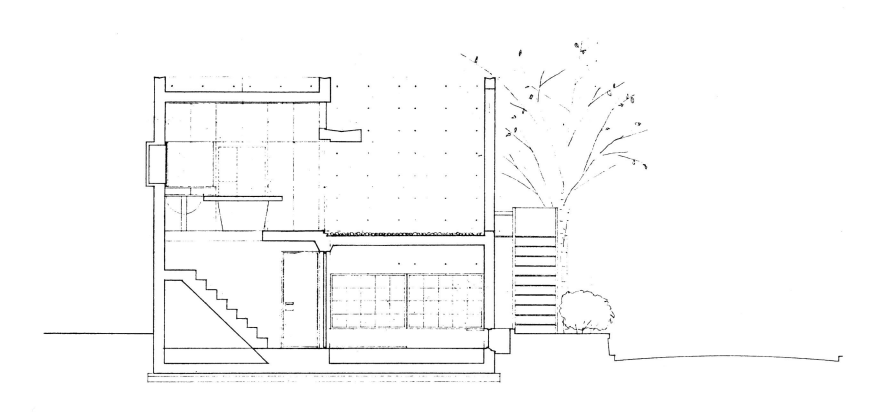

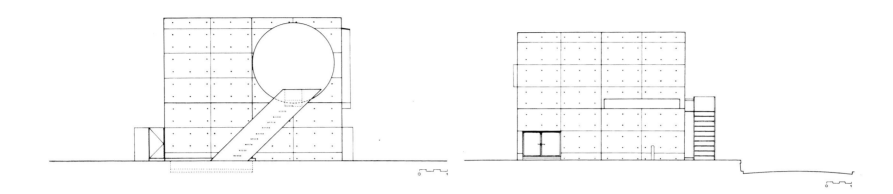

occupies the southern half of the second floor; the other half is the living room/kitchen/dining room separated from the patio only by a series of sliding glass doors.

In contrast to the great opening to the south, the window oriented to the north is long, narrow and located just beneath the roof in order to flood the ceiling with light.

The predominant materials inside are bare concrete and soft-toned wood, the roughness of the former offsetting the latter's polished surfaces.

The bedroom is on the ground floor, to one side of the stair, with a window looking west; the other side accommodates the lavatory and bathroom and, beneath the patio skylight, the tatami room, with the largest opening toward the east, a translucent panel which by toning down the light avoids direct, disturbing contact with the exterior. While the living room above is characterized by a bright, dry atmosphere, its ground-floor counterpart is somewhat dark and humid. Both light and darkness in a house are important to Shirakawa, by virtue above all of the surprises that the contrast is able to produce. As the architect himself states, "It is darkness that allows us to see the light".

The sink, between the table
and wall.

Two views of the tatami room.

The Circle House

The house has no openings to the exterior.
Only its hermeticism is visible
from the city.

This 939 square foot house with an interior square footage of 371 is for an elderly widow. The hospital her husband founded is now run by their two sons, both of whom are doctors. The project is a cylindrical building sited next to the old hospital; the first two floors are an extension of the hospital while the third is the dwelling. Since the setting is not the usual one for a house, unexpected situations are created of overlapping of different functions within the same building, such as the differentiation between the access to the hospital floors and access to the dwelling. Both are related in different ways to the outer layer of the building and with the exterior. While the hospital floors have a continuous line of windows,

the top floor is entirely closed. Half of it is occupied by a garden, onto which all the rooms in the house open. A large glass surface separates this garden from the interior, thus establishing a relationship of transparency between the two. It is nevertheless possible to transform the glass surface by moving some mobile, translucent, paper panels some of these can be closed while others are left open. Partial images of the patio can be obtained in this way, both hiding and revealing views. This, depending on the different lighting, enriches the spatial configurations according to the time of day or the activity being carried out. This flexibility of relationships, possible thanks to the variability of the spaces, also occurs →

View from the street.

The path toward the entry.

between the living room and the tatami room, which can be closed or completely open.

The house has no openings to the exterior. The image of solidity and compactness is accentuated by the dark colouring.

Access to the building is gained gradually: a path leads around it to the entry, from which a covered space continues to the elevator. The moment you leave the elevator, on the dwelling floor, you are still outside the cylinder, but it is now possible to see how to enter it through a cut-out in the circular wall. The door is still not here, however: it is first necessary to cross a patio which provides light and ventilation to the service areas. The interior of the dwelling occupies a rectangular strip and its geometry has been superimposed on the exterior of the building: a rectangle and a circle, simple forms whose intersection provides the project with its layout. Having crossed the patio and a reception hall, you are immediately confronted with a view of the garden. The reception hall is a transitional space situated in a service area for the living room, dining room, bedroom, study and tatami room. This compact →

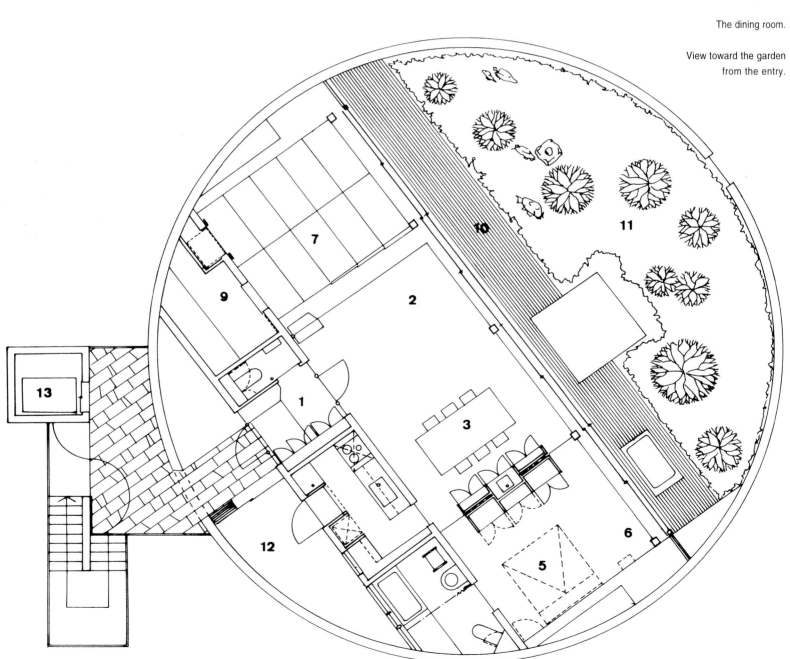

View of the garden.
Detail of the tatami room.

The lavatory.

The bedroom.

View of the garden from the bedroom.

House in Sant Jaume de Sesoliveres

From the very outset a house was planned
that would open to the exterior
and which would be characterized by an ambiguous exterior/interior relationship.

Jaume Riba

Jaume Riba was born in Igualada in 1956. He obtained his degree in architecture in 1982 from the Architecture School of the University of Navarra. Most of his projects have been executed in the Anoia region of the province of Barcelona, for which he has designed houses, commercial and industrial buildings and educational and religious centers.

This project for an open-plan home can be read as a transposition to the present day of Mies van der Rohe's architectural ideas. Some of Mies' houses, and more specifically the pavilion that represented Germany at the 1929 Barcelona World Exhibition, seem to lie behind and inform this work. The project therefore has a markedly referential character, attesting to the possibility of reformulating and revalidating a language or vocabulary established in the recent past of modernism. What is the roof that overhangs the walls, or the walls that cut through space and configure itineraries in their encounter with pure, objective glazed surfaces if not elements in the language of Mies transposed to a contemporary context? Furthermore there is a tendency toward the essential, also characteristic of Mies: thus a bench becomes a piece of pure geometry fixed to a wall

with no aspirations to ornament other than its own texture, while the thin, abstract metal pillars express themselves as pure, objective elements. A basic and typically modern theme developed in this project is the ambiguous interior/exterior relationship. The interior is not a closed space but one that enters into an open relationship with the patio and garden, attaching greater importance to the idea of route and movement than to static space. Global solutions have been sought and careful attention given to the continuity of materials to ensure that the same criteria would be valid for the work as a whole. Thus the ceiling concrete is prolonged to the exterior cantilevers, while certain inside walls extend outside through glass partitions. Moreover, the interior flooring and exterior paving have been treated very similarly.

View of the south facade from the garden.

Two views of the exterior corridor which separates the study and the garage from the rest of the house.

Two details of the south facade, oriented toward the garden. The flat roof is supported on metal pillars while the walls continue up the garden.

Section.

West elevation.

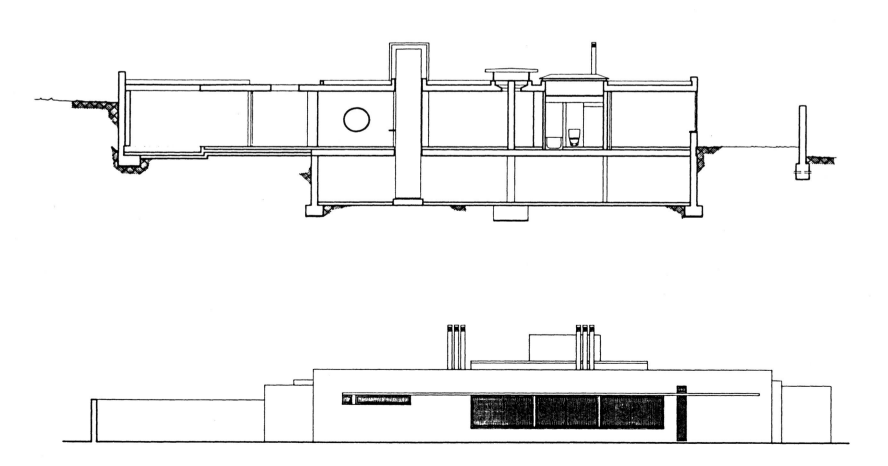

Detail of the pond.

General view of the swimming pool.

The interior space is continuous and unitary: the different rooms with distinct functions are separated by large sliding doors, providing flexibility and permitting the redistribution of space according to the dictates of the moment, of needs or of tastes. The kind of division and re-division that characterizes traditional homes has largely been avoided and the accent placed on the ambiguity of spaces which from the outset were allotted different functions. Thus the house features a hall/dining room/living room, a bedroom/lavatory, a living room/terrace and so on.

The dwelling is schematically divided into three zones. The totally glazed eastern zone contains the living room, dining room, study and library. The western zone, by contrast, is warmer and more protected and contains the bedrooms, the kitchen, the pantry and laundry room.

Finally, the service zone with the shower, bathroom and lavatory is enclosed in a central block, while the washbasins have been placed outside next to freestanding walls that provide a degree of privacy.

The house exterior features the garage and a

A couple of views of the garden.

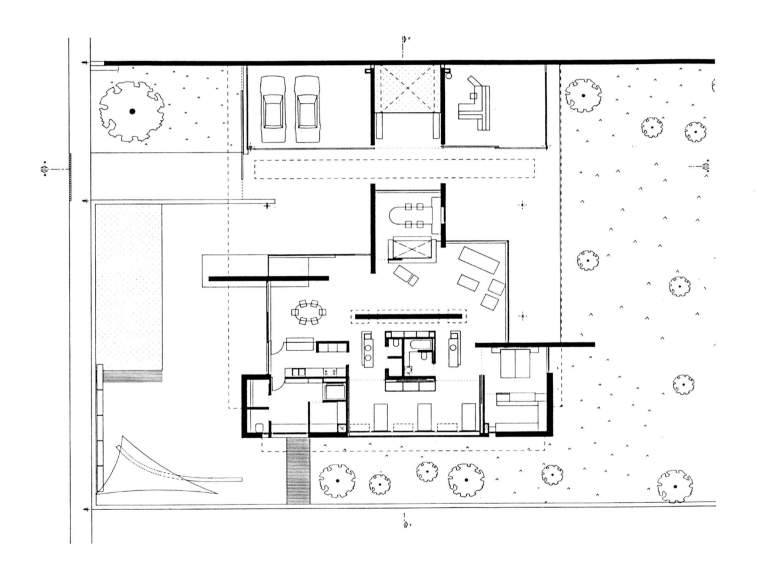

gardening utensils area and workshop facing the living space, linked by the roof, and separated from one another by a pond. The swimming pool, a significant element consisting not only of the rectangular sheet of water but also a curved wall accommodating the changing rooms and drying areas, lies in the northern zone of the site. The ground is paved here, producing a contrast between the more urbanized part and the relatively wild area to the south, marked at one end with a group of large rocks.

This project was conditioned by a number of significant functional and maintenance requirements. To make cleaning easy, potential obstacles on the floor were eliminated (cupboards and wardrobes are built in, the toilets, television and faucets are suspended from the wall, and so on). The surfaces are smooth and clean and facing materials are easy to repair or replace. The installations are completely open and accessible from the basement, so that for most repair jobs there is no need to enter the house as such.

View from the dining room.

The swimming pool lies in the
northern zone of the site.

The interior space is
continuous and unitary.

View of the children's bedroom with the sliding window above the bed-heads.

A living room.

Office.

The washbasin is conceived as a free-standing element supported by the wall.

A specific condition was that the project had to adapt to the physical handicap of one of the family members. Unencumbered movement was therefore essential for a wheelchair and a mechanized wardrobe was also needed so that the person in question could reach clothes from the bed. Clarity in the definition of spaces has been achieved thanks largely to a high degree of mechanization: a rotating filing cabinet holds all the books, a sideways-opening cupboard hides all the toilet utensils, a sliding partition and glass panel provide access to the kitchen table and the sliding outside doors are activated by a pneumatic mechanism.

Practically the whole house is in white concrete, including the flat roof slab. The flooring is of 18 x 18-inch travertine marble tiles with joins one yard apart. The bedroom walls are faced with stained and varnished DM panels while the bathroom, kitchen and washroom surfaces are sheathed in white silica. The central wall is of cross-cut travertine and the outside timber is high-density plywood. The switches, plugs, security alarms, air conditioning and compressed air systems are housed in metal service columns, monitored from a computerized control system.

Different views of the interior.

Detail of the kitchen.

Bom Jesus House

A single-family dwelling consisting of two volumes
that represent two construction systems.
A natural stone block pierces the house.

Eduardo Souto de Moura

Belonging to the so-called "Oporto School", together with Fernando Tavora and Alvaro Siza Vieira, the works of Souto de Moura (Oporto, 1952) reveal special concern for analyzing the context, both as a physical-environmental factor or as a cultural factor, as well as for the re-interpretation of traditional construction techniques and the use of simple, austere formal language. Its principle achievements reflect the search for an abstraction which reflects the components of location and use. His first major project, the Braga Municipal Market (1980 - 1984), confirms the use which Souto de Moura makes of a formal neoplastic language that establishes a link with Mies van der Rohe, later applying it to the reality of the project. Outstanding examples of his work are the Cultural Center for the S.E.C. (Oporto, 1981 - 1988), the Earth Sciences Department at the University of Aveiro (1990 - 1994) and the project for a hotel in Salzburg (1987).

A gently-sloping stone path approaches the house, situated on the upper part of the site.

An exterior stone stair, perpendicular to the main facade, links the upper terrace with the access level.

Houses constitute an outstanding aspect of Souto de Moura's work in that they are true prodigies of sensitivity to social and environmental contexts. His House 1 (1982 - 1985) and House 2 (1983 -1988) in Nevogilde, Oporto, the house for the Quinta do Lago (Algarve, 1984 - 1989), the house in Alcanena (Torres Novas, 1987 - 1992) and the house in Miramar (Villa Nova de Gaia, 1987 -1991), are all compositions of great formal simplicity by no means at odds with the quality of life enjoyed in their interiors.

The conceptual and linguistic simplicity exemplified by the Bom Jesus House, a single-family home on the outskirts of Braga, is a clear example of how to respond adequately and subtly to an existing physical environment, to a local cultural and artisan tradition and to specific program requirements.

Initial sketches on the basis of which the project was subsequently developed.

The composition of the house is a symbiosis between two construction and cultural systems; between a concrete and glass cube and a cube of granite.

Following pages:
The terracing produced by the stone volume creates a garden opposite the main facade.

The northeast facade of the dwelling, where the stone wall creates a platform with a more private rear space on the edge of the site.

The lower granite volume bonds the concrete and glass body, which contains the main dependencies of the dwelling, with the terrain.

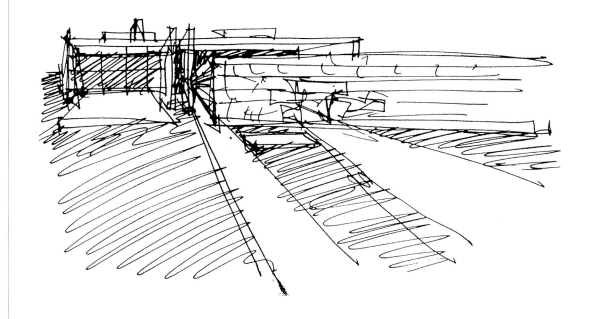

The parti consists of two units representing two programs and two different construction systems, combining two houses in the same project. The natural stone block that runs through the house and the concrete and glass cube resting on the platform that delimits the stone wall symbolize the encounter between the old and the new. Through an interplay of dualities the composition integrates with its surroundings and creates a succession of physically and visually linked interior and exterior spaces.

The Bom Jesus House stands on a site with a pronounced slope to the southwest, oriented toward the uneven silhouette of the city of Braga. The stone-paved approach climbs gently, almost ritualistically, up to the dwelling on the upper limit of the site.

By virtue of its decomposition into two complementary volumes, the house bonds itself with the orography of the site. The natural stone cube constituting the first floor is the prolongation of an exterior wall which, echoing the unevenness of the terrain, produces a terracing at top-floor level and a gently-sloping garden in front of →

The northwest facade of the dwelling reveals the abstract presence of the concrete cube, which stands out white against the landscape.

Preliminary sketch.

Site plan.

Ground-floor plan.

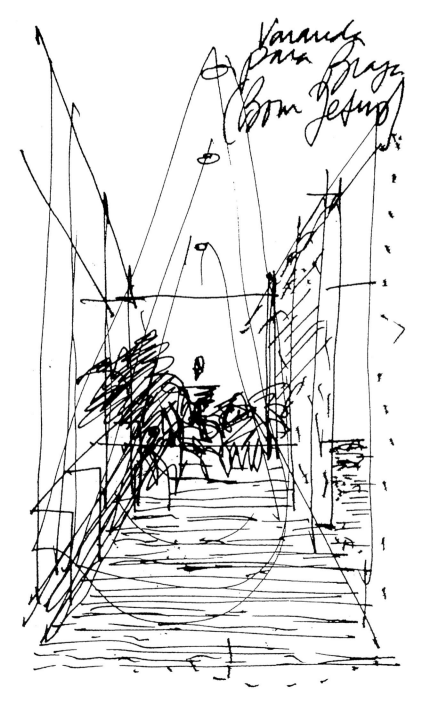

the first floor. This reflects a desire to mimic the natural stone walls around the site, characteristic of rural zones in the region. This granite wall, pierced by the doors and windows of the first-floor dependencies, crosses transversally through a whitewashed concrete cube, with completely glazed southwest and northeast facades, creating another exterior space at the rear of the house on the same level as the upper terrace.

The white cube, perhaps the project's most striking feature, straddles the first-floor and top levels, constituting an abstract element that stands in special empathy with the granite wall. Its side facades are completely transparent while the long facades are thoroughly opaque, linking the exterior with the interior and providing the first-floor rooms with access to each other.

The compositional and constructional duality of the Bom Jesus House has a corresponding duality in the program. On the ground floor, the stone unit contains the service areas, boiler room and garage, together with a games room designed mainly for children and a guest room, all in direct contact with the garden, located in front of the main facade, thanks to the openings in the granite wall.

A double-height entrance hall within the concrete volume, completely glazed at its ends and paved with ceramic tiles which extend to the exterior, leads to the dwelling level via a light metallic stair with wooden steps. On this level the bedrooms, the living room and the dining

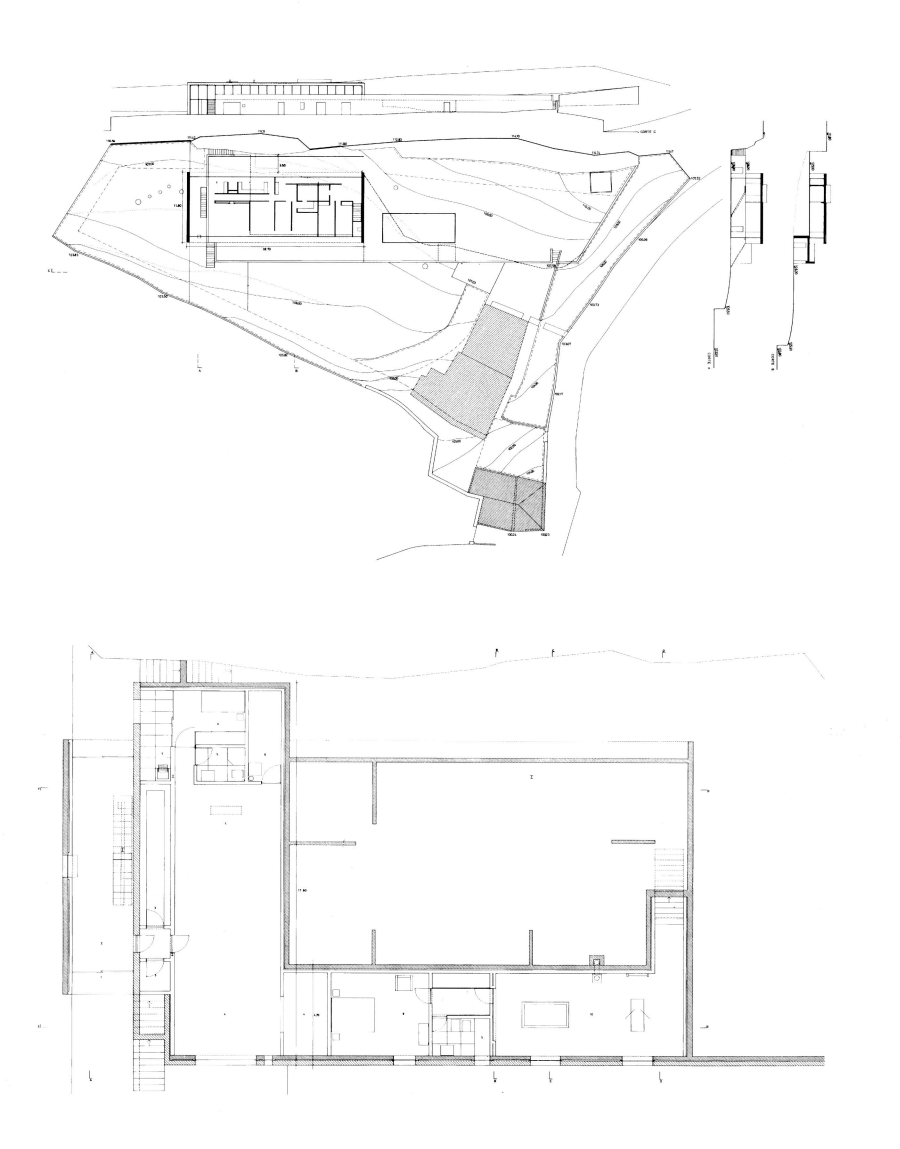

A large timber-paved terrace-
belvedere rises opposite the
glazed southwest facade of the
upper level of the house.

The stone wall terraces the
terrain, creating an upper garden
platform in direct contact with
the dwelling's dependencies.

A prism rises above the roof,
providing the top-floor bath-
rooms with overhead light.

Plan of the second floor.

Following pages:

Cross sections.
Longitudinal sections.

The stone cube which
constitutes the lower volume of
the house mimics the walls that
surround the site.

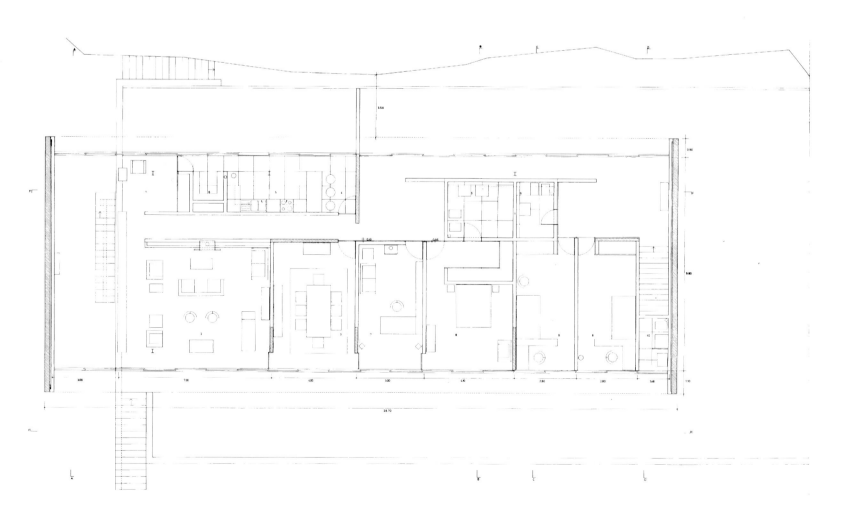

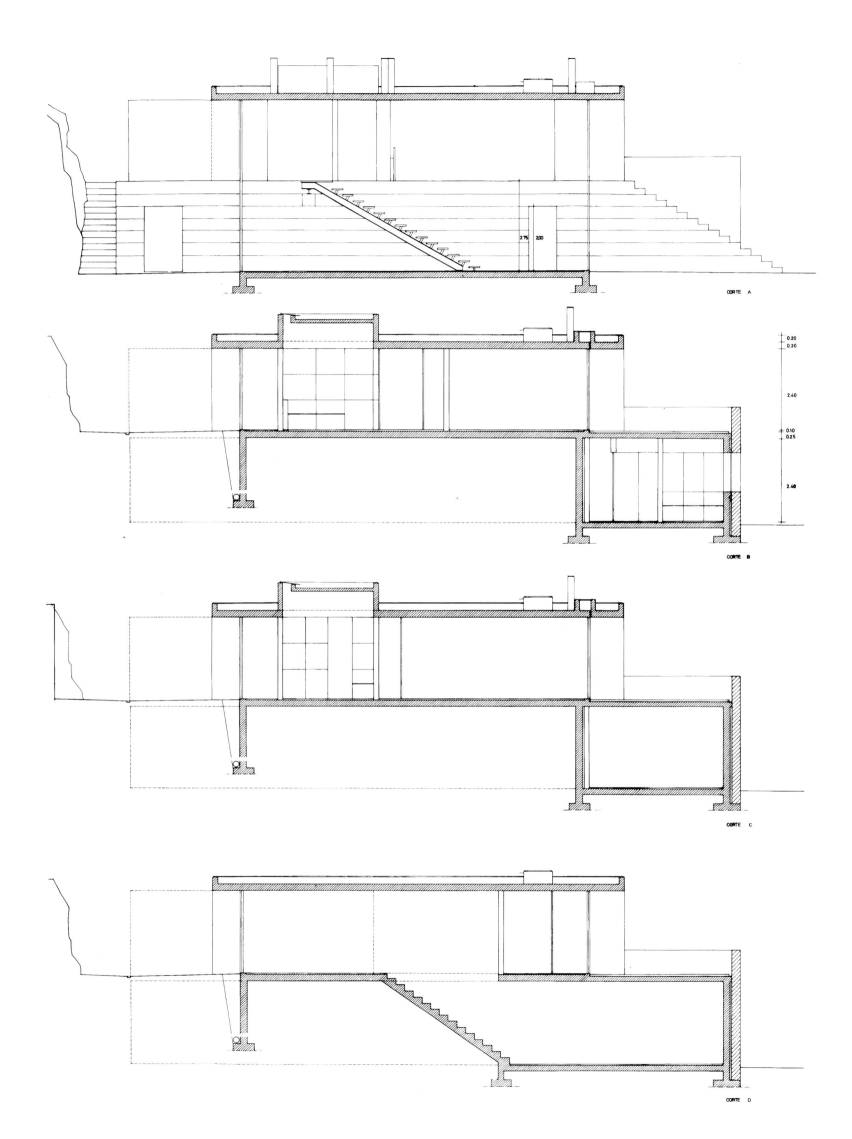

CORTE A

CORTE B

0.20
0.20
2.40
0.10
0.25
2.40

CORTE C

CORTE D

2.75 2.00

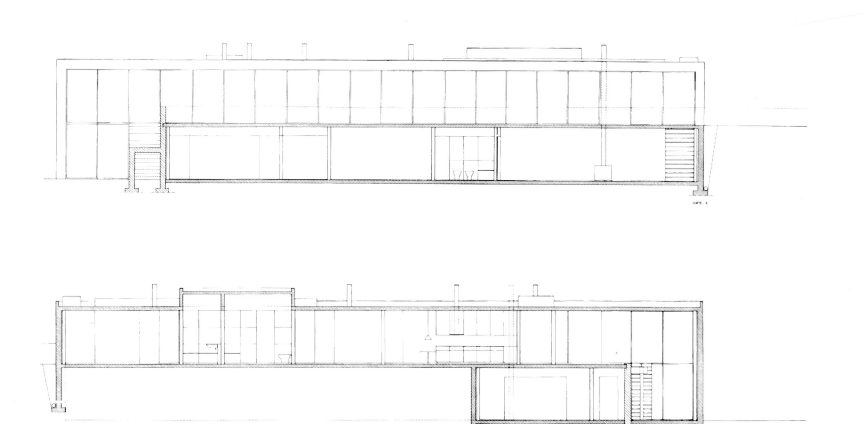

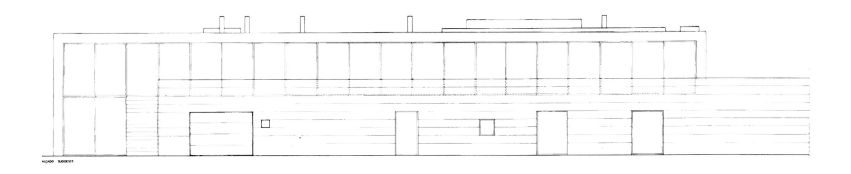

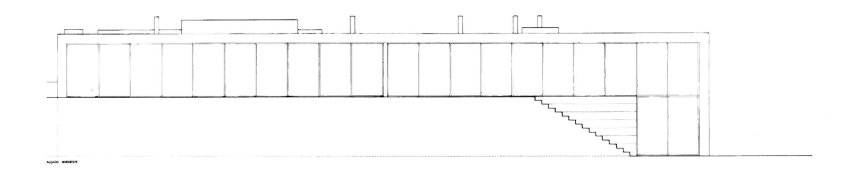

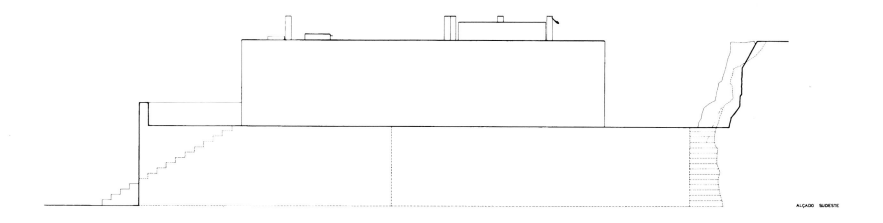

ALÇADO SUDESTE

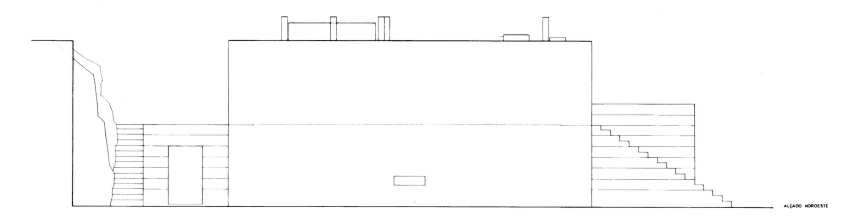

ALÇADO NOROESTE

Natural materials such as granite or wood combine with the glass or unpainted aluminum of the exterior carpentry.

The granite wall with openings recalls traditional constructions in the rural zones of Portugal.

Southwest and northeast facades.

room extend along the length of the southwest facade, in time with the precise rhythm marked by the unpainted aluminum exterior carpentry, which also determines the rhythm of the structure. All these dependencies enjoy direct access to the timber-paved terrace stretching in front of them to the natural garden created by the terracing on the same level, where the swimming pool is sited. A stone stair next to the lower wall and perpendicular to the facade connects this terrace-belvedere to the lower garden. The kitchen looks northeast and is connected to a more pri-

vate exterior zone at the rear of the house, directly linked in turn to the lower level by means of a natural stone stair.

The distribution of this upper floor permits smooth links between the spaces, while at the same time clearly delimiting them. The structure, a combination of steel pillars and concrete screens, adapts its rhythm and arrangement to this limitation of spaces and to the direct communication of all these with the exterior through the large inset french windows in the concrete cube's long facades.

The use of natural materials, such as the granite of the lower volume, the varnished beech wood of the doors and interior panelling, the top-floor wood parquet or the Alentejo ceramic paving of the first floor, is a characteristic not only specific to this house but also common to all Souto de Moura's projects.

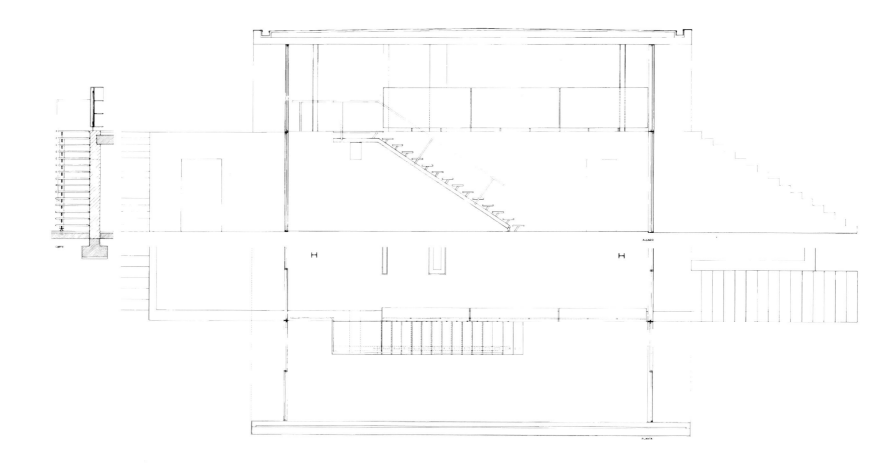

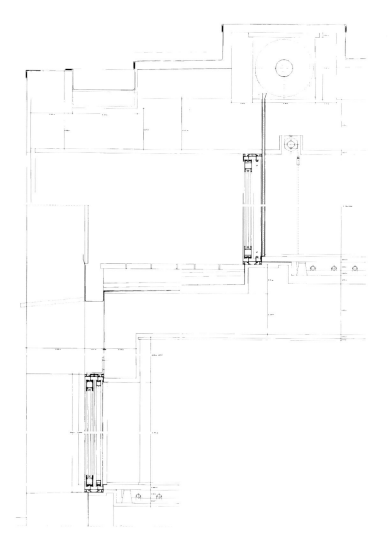

Detail of the stair in the double-height access space.

Detail of the support of the metal and wood staircase parallel to the stone wall in the entrance hall.

The aluminum carpentry of the double-height entrance space separates the interior and exterior where the granite wall penetrates the house.

This page.

Construction detail of the facade.

The interior of the living room extends toward the exterior terrace with views over the city of Braga.

Following pages:

The spatial continuity of the interior communal areas is prolonged toward the exterior thanks to the large glazed facades.

The double-height entrance hall is presided over by a light metallic stair that contrasts with the imposing natural stone wall.

Amat House

A house based on the memory of its predecessor.
Although for two families,
it is not two separate dwellings.

Antoni de Moragas

Antoni de Moragas (Barcelona, 1941) studied at the Barcelona University Arts Faculty and at the Barcelona School of Architecture. He has worked in the Ricardo Bofill Architecture Workshop and in the studios of Martorell/Bohigas/Mackay, Barcelona, and Vittorio Gregotti, Milan. He is currently Projects Professor at the Barcelona School of Architecture and at the EINA School. In 1987 his Gay House was awarded the FAD prize for architecture and in 1993 his Amat House received special mention.

The Amat House is on the same site as and replaces the Amat family's former summer residence. The owners were very familiar with the place: the effects of the different orientations, the old swimming pool, the trees, the neighbors. Memories of the old house and past habits form part of the new project: outdoor meals in the shade, the clear light of springtime in the garden, the trees, the shortest way out to the surrounding streets. Like a chest, the house was required to store memories of childhood.

The house is in fact for the families of two broth-ers; it had to be possible for only one to live there, both in winter and summer, or for the two families together, though never thinking in terms of two separate dwellings. Actually, the house would be much the same if it were for a single family: the dining room, kitchen and living room are communal and the bedrooms, on the floor above, are identical to each other.

The site is practically square and almost flat, although on a different level from the plot next door. This difference in height made it possible to include a basement, which contains the →

Site plan.
View from the swimming area.

View from the street.

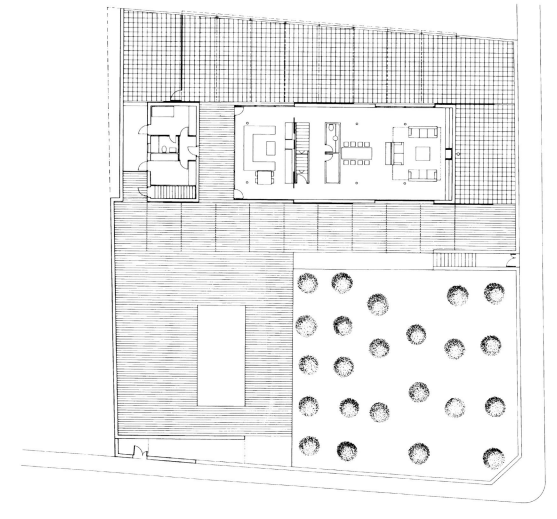

garage, entered from the street to the east, together with a series of rooms for different uses and services.

The house is organised inside a thoroughly regular volume, a two-floor box stretching from the eastern to the western ends of the site. A tunnel passes through the building and links the north and south gardens, to be enjoyed alternately during the year, one in winter and the other in summer. Beside a clump of trees in the southern section lies the old rectangular swimming pool, conceived as a sheet of water cut into a surface of timber. Tree plantings have been maintained in the section of the site overlooking the crossroads as a complement to the pool.

Next to the tunnel, and separated from it by a glazed partition, is the kitchen area, a large light-flooded space delimited on one side by the stair wall and on the remaining three completely open to the exterior, garden and rear patio.

The house is wide enough inside to accommodate the single-flight stair crosswise. Next to it, Antoni de Moragas has placed another transversal element, a freestanding volume containing →

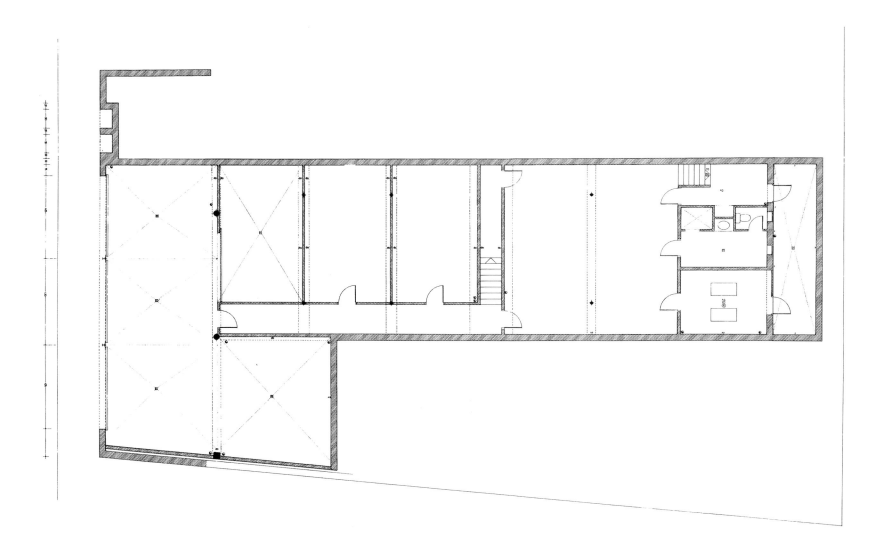

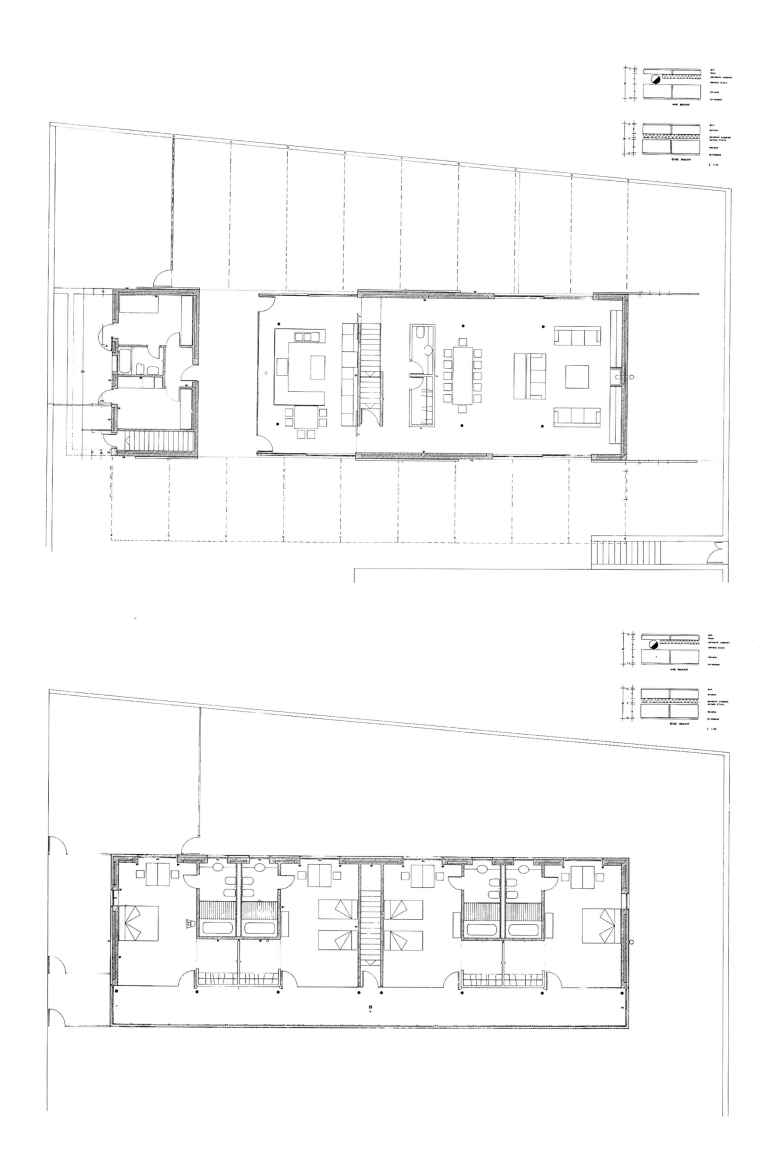

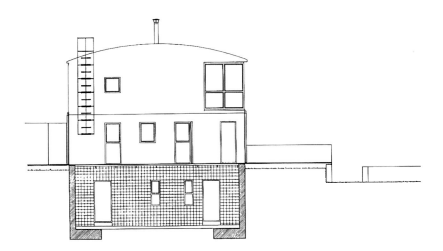

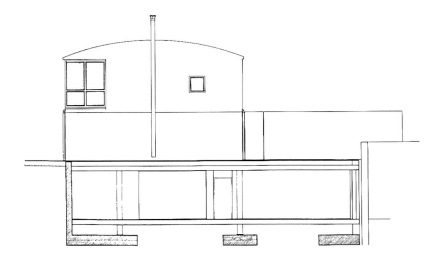

a small lavatory and a cloakroom, the function of which is to separate the stair from the dining and living rooms, which are flooded with light thanks to the large openings to the exterior on both sides.

In the south section a porch runs along the whole length of the building, providing protection from excess light; the light that does filter through draws different textures on the warm-colored walls whose tones range from ocher through yellow to red.

On the other side of the tunnel opposite the →

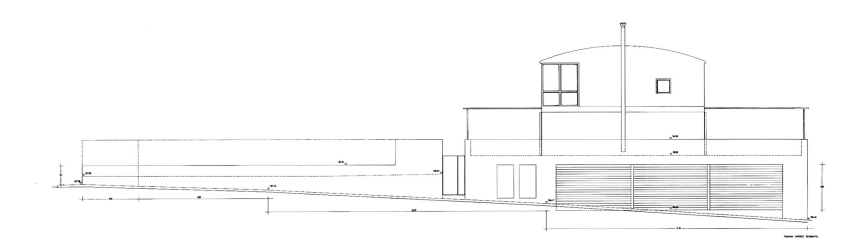

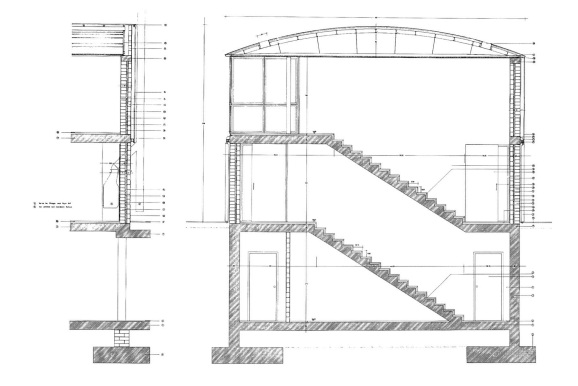

East elevation.

Section through the
staircase.

View of the east facade.

kitchen is a practically enclosed volume containing two small bedrooms and a bathroom and
opening onto a patio that lies between the end
of the house and the site limit.

The two master bedrooms with private bath-
rooms and dressing rooms are on the second
floor, together with two double bedrooms, sym-
metrically placed with respect to the others, each
again with its own bathroom and dressing room.
They all give onto a large open verandah,
although they also have windows looking north,
toward the rear of the house. →

Views of the porch from different angles. In the first, the south facade.

The cane structure that forms the porch.

View of the kitchen from the porch.

The slight curve of the copper roof is almost imperceptible when the house is seen from the front, though it is much more obvious from the side facades. The walls are of sheathed painted brick on the first floor and faced with wood panels on the floor above. Both the sliding and fixed windows feature carpentry in galvanized iron.

The garden paving consists of timber specially treated for outdoor wear and is slightly raised above the lawn.

The architect discovered a secret about this house: on a wall remaining from the old construction, which had hitherto remained hidden, someone had drawn a hieroglyph one summer. Perhaps its mystery will soon be transmitted to the new house.

General view of the
living room.

Following pages:

The kitchen area.

View of the dining room
and its furnishings.

The stair access area.

The Charlotte House

This house is one of the few examples
of dwellings designed by Günter Behnisch.
An unusual case,
since it is actually the Behnisch family residence.

Behnisch & Partner

Günter Behnisch was born in Dresden in 1922 and studied at the Stuttgart Technische Hochschule, graduating in 1951. In 1952 he set up his own architecture studio where he worked with Bruno Lambart until 1958. In 1966 he began his collaboration with architects F. Auer, W. Büxel, E. Tränkner, K. Weber and M. Sabatke, finally setting up Behnisch & Partner (Behnisch, Büxel, Sabatke and Tränkner).

From 1967 until 1987, the year in which he retired from teaching, he was Director of the Building Standards Institute at the Darmstadt Technische Hochschule, where he also gave design and planning classes.

He is member of the International Academy of Architecture, Sofia (1990), an honorary member of the Royal Incorporation of Architects in Scotland, Edinburgh (1992) and of the Royal Institute of British Architects, London (1995) as well as a founder member of the Sächsische Akademie der Künste in Dresden.

The Charlotte House is an exceptional project far from typical of Behnisch & Partner's usual work. During the forty-five years since the creation of the studio in 1952, Behnisch and his team have entered over four hundred architectural competitions and executed over one hundred projects, a truly impressive list from which, strangely enough, the housing theme is conspicuously absent. Only the occasional porter's lodge as part of a much larger construction or perhaps a block of apartments for rent. The team are much more involved with public or social building projects such as the Ulm Engineering School (1958), the first public building in Germany to be built completely from prefabricated elements; the Munich Olympic Sports Complex (1972), in collaboration with Frei Otto and the Leonhardt and Andrä engineering firm, for which by using his translucent membrane technology Behnisch developed the topology concept that earned him international recognition; the German Parliament building in Bonn and a wide range of kindergartens, schools, institutes, old peoples homes, council buildings and congress centers. His schools, based on the extensive use of prefabricated systems, are considered exemplary institutional buildings, major examples of which are the Hohenstaufen Gymnasium in Göppigen (1959), the Mittelpunktschule in Oppelsbohm (1969), and the Mittelschule (1973) and Hauptschule (1982) in Schaefersfeld. Practically all these buildings are the result of the team's successful participation in competitions.

While broadly speaking Behnisch's first works →

The facade overlooking the
street, characterized by a
transparency that rejects
any radical split between
interior and exterior. In this
case the transparency is
directional, determined by
the shape of the roof.

Detail of the roof above the
trees.

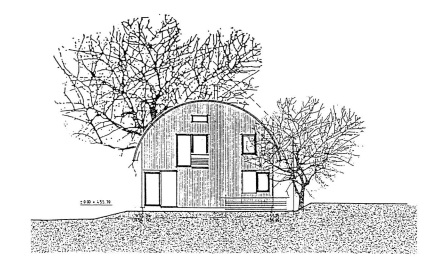

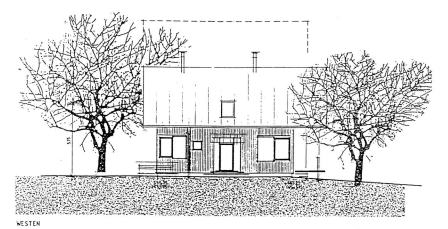

WESTEN

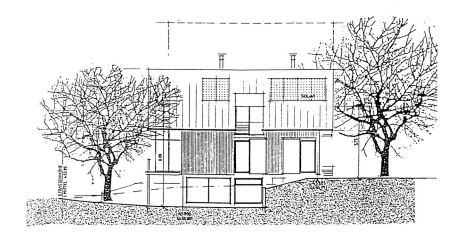

Detail of the model of the house,
in which the clear differentiation
between levels can
be appreciated.

The house is situated in quite a
densely populated area of relatively
small plots.

Rear and side elevations.

Partial view of the facade, which
reveals
attention to materials
and detail.

were informed by a Cartesian-style system in which all the project elements were governed by a logic of modules and standardized dimensions, his more recent projects are characterized by greater complexity based on the superimposition of different systems and greater freedom of associations: complex organic compositions that in some cases include a high degree of fragmentation. Take, for example, the Hysolar Research Institute, University of Stuttgart (1987) and the Luginsland kindergarten (1990).

On the fringe, however, of any possible evolution or transformations in Behnisch's work, there is one constant concern: to discover the spirit of the site. Architecture of place and situation (Situationsarchitectur) as opposed to the imposition of external laws, of absolute abstract principles which, for Behnisch, are invariably violent in their effect. His projects are founded on the particular, on the extraordinary qualities of a single event, rather than on totalizing visions.

In this sense, the architecture of Behnisch & Partner clearly represents the impetus and values of German democracy. It is a pluralist architec- →

The access, on the side, reached by climbing some steps.

Detail of the entrance landing, where brightly coloured mosaic tiles have been incrusted in the terrazzo.

Southwest elevation.

Cross section.

ture that seeks difference, not uniformity, as something capable of defining an order. And for Behnisch this internal order of the things of Mankind is a metaphor for the order to which society aspires: difference and diversity as the solid foundations of all relationships fit perfectly into this framework.

In the last analysis, the central point of his architecture is the principle of a complex, organized unity, the synthesis of multiple elements. Furthermore, this tendency toward unity emerges from under a relative disorder, seen as a reflection of the very complexity of reality.

Sillenbuch is a Stuttgart suburb situated on land rising above the city, near the Silberwald forest, and characterized by single-family houses with gable roofs. While some of these were built in the thirties, most are from after 1950 and feature gray half-barrel roofs with solar energy panels.

For different reasons there is a lack of available building land in Stuttgart and her hinterland, a fact which has given rise to a variety of problems. Among these is the high price of land and the consequent need to design houses to fit into

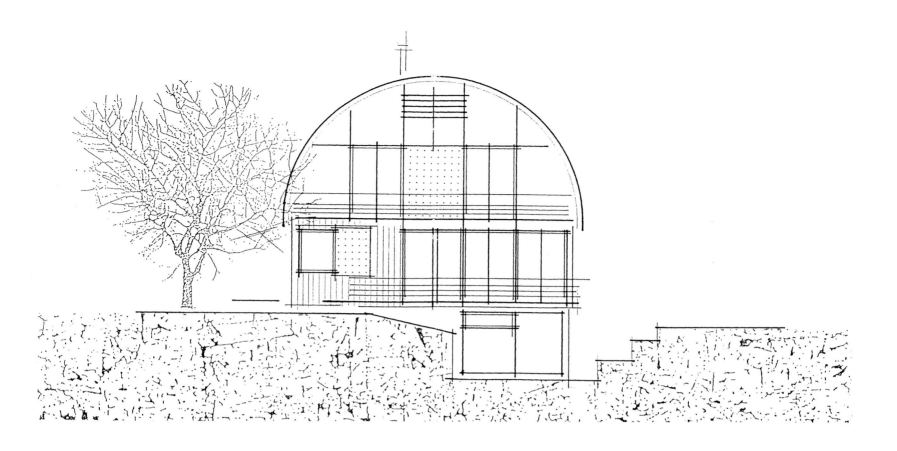

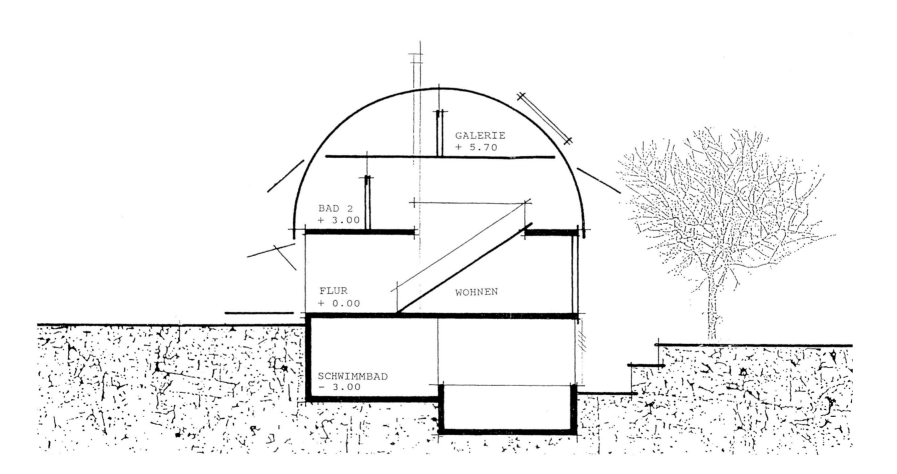

GALERIE
+ 5.70

BAD 2
+ 3.00

FLUR
+ 0.00

WOHNEN

SCHWIMMBAD
− 3.00

View of the dining-
living room from the stair. In
the background, the terrace
with timber-board paving and
the bench, which also serves as
a handrail.

small plots. In the case of the Charlotte House, the area available was only 1,313 square feet, and once regulations for the control of distances had been taken into account there was room only for a cube in the center of the rectangular site. For circumstantial reasons an elevator was also necessary, as well as special dimensions and installations in all the rooms. The house design also had to allow for separation of the upper floors so that they could be rented. On the other hand, howe-

ver, these determining factors could not reduce the potential qualities that all independent, single-family houses should possess. As a family residence, the house had to be comfortable and a source of different impressions and sensations. A small swimming pool was also necessary, and the house had to be constructed in such a way that the materials, elements and systems employed had the minimum possible impact on the environment and inhabitants. In other words,

By extending onto
the terrace, the living
area partially forms part
of the exterior.

The kitchen opens into
the dining room, forming
a flowing
uncompartmented space.

In the foreground, detail
of the fireplace and a
small portion of the living
area.
In the background,
the kitchen.

the principles of biological architecture had to be fully respected. For this reason, ecologically "friendly" materials were used, such as paints and lacquers produced from natural resins. Neither the wooden floor nor the cupboards have been sealed, but waxed and treated with oil. None of the wood has been protected by chemical products. This ecological approach to the project is nothing new to Behnisch, for in the Munich Stadium he had already examined from a different perspective the feasibility of co-existence between the natural and the artificial. In that case, structural engineers collaborated with landscape architects.

The kitchen, dining room and living area are on the ground floor, together constituting a large non-subdivided space which, if necessary, can be linked to a work area by a sliding partition. The rooms on the next two floors are already inside the semi-cylindrical roof. The subterranean floor, the biological basement, with installations and the swimming pool, receives light from the south since the site topology made openings possible here.

The Charlotte House is rich in images and in attention to detail and, like all of Behnisch's architecture, has to be explored inside to be understood. Aesthetic analysis is of little use compared to direct experience of its spaces and passages, of its different colors and textures.

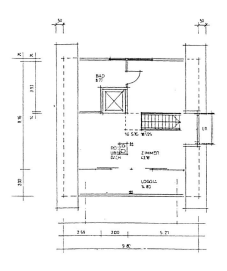

Through the french windows one sees that the surrounding houses are completely different.

Clockwise: the attic floor, the second floor, the first floor and basement.

DACHGESCHOSS

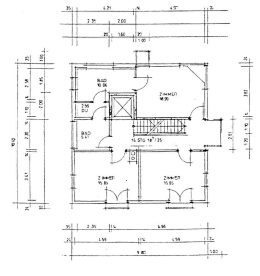

OBERGESCHOSS

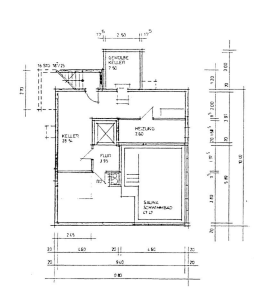

KELLERGESCHOSS

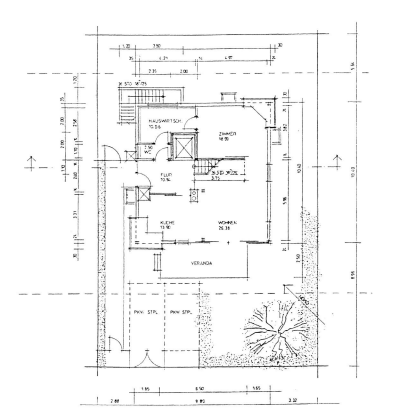

Wood finishes dominate the interior, in both the flooring and the furniture.
The architect has by no means rejected the possibility of introducing traditional furniture.

The wood has been treated with natural oils rather than protected with chemical products.

Detail of the handrail. The
staircase is supported by a
light structure.

A bedroom within the space
enclosed by the roof.

The southwest bedrooms have
a full-length balcony.

Access to the attic from the
two bedrooms is by means of
a steep light
staircase.

Detail of the attic, one
of the most unusual features
of the house.

Häusler House

Its strict geometrical form contrasts
with the untamed landscape,
over which a few houses have been scattered

Karl Baumschlager & Dietmar Eberle

Karl Baumschlager (Bregenz, Vorarlberg, 1956) studied at the Hochschule für Angewandte Kunst, where he was a student of H. Hollein, W. Holzbauer and O. M. Ungers; he graduated in 1982.
Dietmar Eberle (Hittisau, Bregenzerwald, Vlb., 1952) studied at the Vienna Higher Technical College; he was a teacher at the Hannover TU from 1982 to 1986 and at the Vienna TU from 1983 to 1989. Since 1984 he has worked with Karl Baumschlager, and together they won the Austrian Dwelling Prize in 1986. From 1991 to 1994 he was guest professor at the Zurich ETH and, in 1994, at Syracuse University, New York.

The Häusler House is a single-family dwelling on a flat, open site in Hard, Austria, whose strictly geometric form contrasts with the untamed landscape, over which a few buildings are scattered here and there without following any pre-established order.

As a building it was deliberately designed to be different from those around it, mostly nondescript, practically identical single-family houses with gable roofs, lacking any clear mutual relationship or any link with the landscape.

By contrast, the Häusler House possesses a clear, imposing conceptual form, consisting essentially of a rectangular volume which unashamedly displays its rugged texture of unfaced gray concrete, and within which the project develops.

The access and side facades are practically closed to the exterior, only the south side being completely open. This facade consists of a regular concrete structure which establishes a uniform screen, behind which different more or less staggered planes of wooden sheets appear.

The access facade to the north is a gray concrete rectangle whose only compositional elements are the entry recess and a long, narrow, horizontal window on the right that reaches the corner. There is an evident contrast between these two faces, which clearly determine front and rear, the latter closed and the former open to take full advantage of the best available views. →

View from the east.

West facade.

South facade.

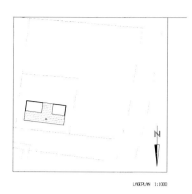

LAGEPLAN 1:1000

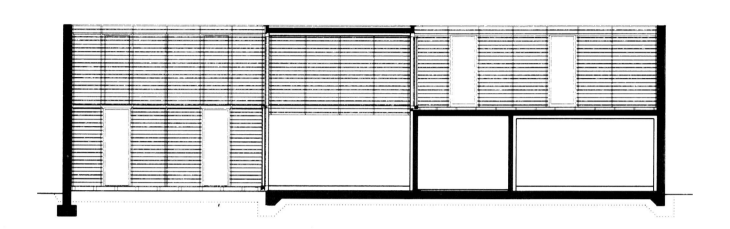

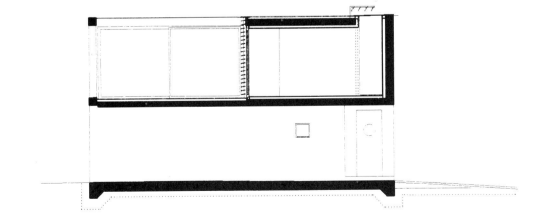

The two side facades are hermetic: the one looking west has a central opening, from top to bottom and divided into four, while the east facade features a smaller, off-center opening through which light penetrates the bedroom of a small rented apartment included in the house and isolated from the rest on the eastern side of the ground floor.

The house recalls Donald Judd's concrete sculptures: pure, geometric forms of large dimensions standing in open landscapes and establishing a strange, disconcerting order. Similarly, the Baumschlager and Eberle house appears as a forceful, impenetrable, indecipherable object. Nevertheless, both the narrow openings in the blind concrete walls and the second skin of wood that remains exposed on the south facade reveal that a different law governs the interior, one of intimate, warm spaces enhanced and tempered by the different light qualities.

The project began with a series of emptying operations: the rectangular volume was subjected to successive subtractions in the form of recesses converted into terraces on both →

floors. These are empty spaces of air and light; open, exterior spaces that organize the different suites and rooms. Thanks to this emptying operation, the interior spaces are well lit and spacious while an interesting relationship is established between the exterior and the interior through these outside transition spaces which are nonetheless encompassed by the exterior concrete shell.

The entry to the house and the itineraries through its different spaces are understood as gradual displacements from a closed element to a spacious, open, interior. The entrance area on the north facade is produced by an axis which pierces the building perpendicularly and from which access is gained to the three separate units which make up the dwelling. To the east is the small rented apartment; its square footage of almost 164 accommodates a south-facing living room and, at the rear, a bedroom looking east and a bathroom ventilated from the entrance area. The summer house, a small, rectangular, abstract-looking hermetic timber room that seems to have been expelled from the main building, stands at the end of the axis that runs through the house. The outer skin, mostly of bare concrete, has been faced with wood at the entry in order to enhance the importance of this area. To the west is the entry to the main dwelling, with a square footage of 571 (the total square footage is 755). Access is gained from the side, immediately after leaving behind a service area, complete with lavatory, beside the door.

Following on from the access area is the dining room and kitchen, a space completely open to the south, into which light filters through the →

timber-slat facing featured at different points of the project. Another long narrow window looks northwards. This arrangement of openings creates a sensation of transparency without upsetting the duality of opacity and transparency established between the two facades. Next to the dining room, and on the other side of the terrace, is the living room with a double-height ceiling; a lengthwise stair rises up from the dining room and reaches the bedroom floor, which occupies the rear part of the dwelling only. This floor has no passageways, the bedrooms being arranged on both sides of a freestanding block containing the stair and the bathroom.

The living room.

View from one of the bedrooms.

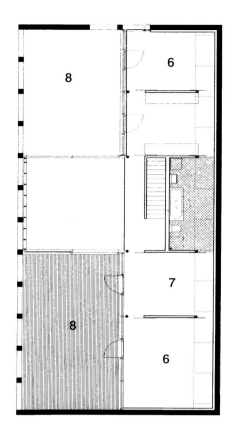

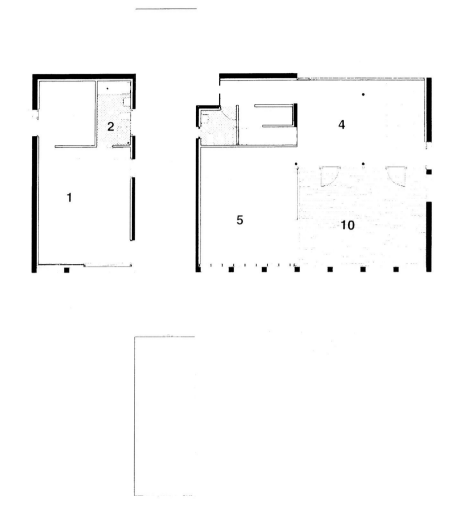

The bathroom.

The first floor:
rented
apartment; bathroom;
lavatory; dining room and
kitchen; living room;
terrace.

The second floor
bathroom; bedroom;
dressing room;
empty space.

Burger House

In a way, and in relation to the topography,
the construction of the house implies
a double operation of opposite characteristics:
the excavation of an empty volume and the construction of a solid one.

Karl Baumschlager and
Dietmar Eberle

The south facade from the
street.

Detail of the south terrace.

The city of Bregenz marks the presence of Austria on border-forming Lake Constance, which the country shares with Germany and Switzerland. The Burger residence stands on a site sloping steeply south-north and enjoying views of the lake.

The building is very simple, its ground plan almost a perfect rectangle (20 x 30 feet), and consists of four floors, the lowest of which is half-buried. Access is from the south by means of a ramp which climbs gently up to an intermediate floor that accommodates the entrance hall, guest lavatory, master bedroom and bathroom.

The floor immediately below is for the children. It contains a north-facing bathroom, a central play area and two bedrooms with direct access to the south patio, excavated from the ground and defined by an exterior retaining wall. In a way, →

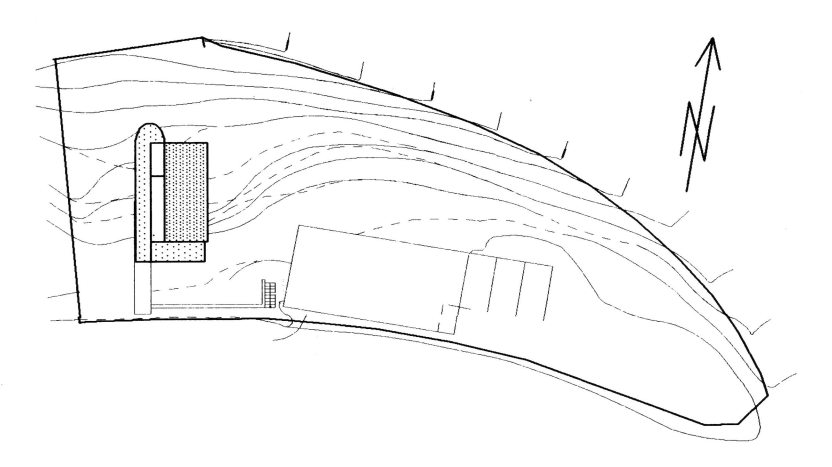

Topographical site plan.

The east facade: laws governing a modulated plan set in nature.

The access floor:
bathroom
hall
bedroom
lavatory
The first floor and patio:
bedroom
games room

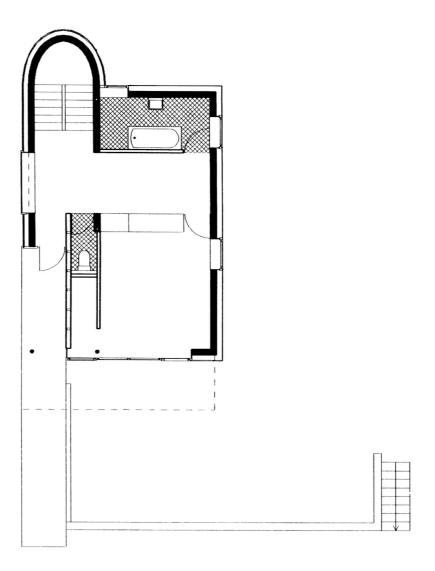

and in relation to the topography, the construction of the house implies a double operation of opposing characteristics: the excavation of an empty volume and the construction of a solid one. Both volumes are similar in size and geometry: straight, bold lines which introduce a distinct, forceful shape into the middle of the rambling forest.

On the top floor the kitchen, dining room and living room are brought together in the same space. The work surfaces of the kitchen constitute a strip along the whole length of the west wall. A large linear skylight provides the illumination for this space, at the same time marking the difference between the distinct areas on the top floor. Likewise, a terrace at the entrance facade and a large, north-facing window with views over the lake flood this space with light. Due to the slope of the site, this floor appears to be at ground level when seen from the street, while from the north slope it rises four stories above ground.

The layout is conceived on the basis of the section and the uses distributed among relatively small floors. In the Burger residence, the characteristics of each space are different from those of more conventional types of dwellings. Thus →

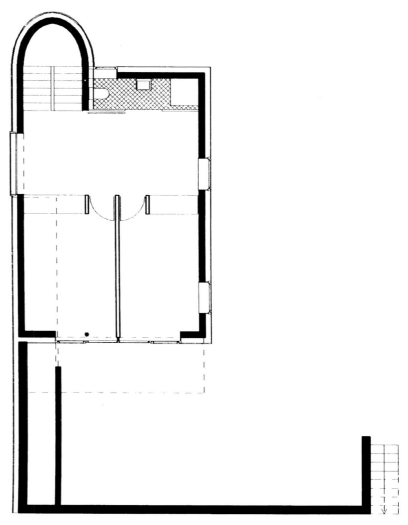

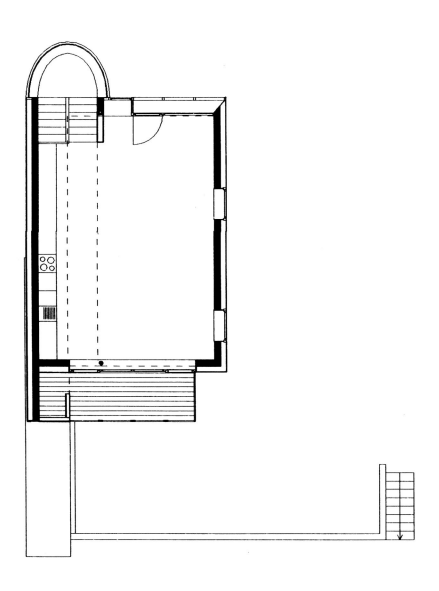

The top floor:
living room,
kitchen and dining room.

Section through the patio
and the stair.

The brick body, with the
entry, the double-height window and the transparent top
floor.

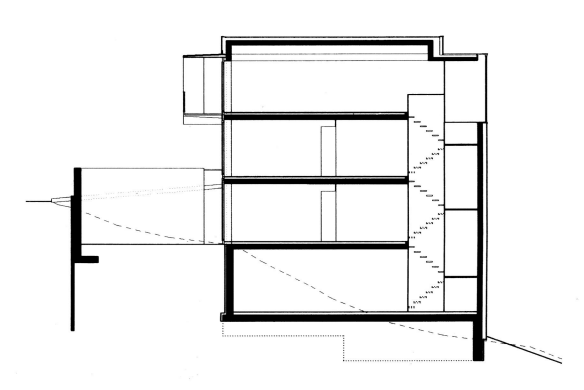

the service space in the semi-basement is a kind of loft or attic, whereas what would normally be the second floor has been placed at the top to take advantage of the views over the lake. The distribution of uses on different floors means that the light can be treated differently on each. This influences the arrangement of the openings and, by extension, the composition of the facades. Perhaps one of the most surprising aspects of this house is its external appearance. The differing characters of the wall sections, depending on their orientation, and the contrast of materials respond to a certain extent to the variety of functions of the interior spaces.

Thus the openings in the west facade correspond to the itineraries inside the building: the entrance space, the large double-height window, the opening on the top floor, at the end of the stair. The chosen material is brick and, by virtue of the curve of the stair, in appearance the house is reminiscent of some of the hermetic projects of Expressionism, one of the most neglected episodes of the international modern style.

There are hardly any openings on the north

The simple master bedroom complete with curtains for privacy.

From the landing it is possible to see the front door, the skylight and the facade itself.

The kitchen, the living-dining room and a second balcony.

facade, only on the top floor, four stories above ground. Forty feet of blind wall with large windows above: from this perspective, the house looks like a watchtower.

The composition of the east facade is geometric and minimalist, with tall narrow windows which perfectly match the quartering of the yellow-painted plywood elements. The south facade is the most open. The large bedroom windows relate to the private patio dug out of the ground and isolated from the street by the retaining wall.

House in Sakuragoaka

The house design was determined by a series
of existing factors: the topography, the orientation,
and local urban planning regulations.

Kunihiko Hayakawa

Born in Tokyo in 1941, Kunihiko Hayakawa studied architecture at the University of Waseda, Takenaka Komuten, Tokyo, and followed a post-graduate course at the Yale University School of Architecture. Kunihiko Hayakawa Architect and Associates, Tokyo, was set up in 1978.

"The City and the Gaze" is a text by Hayakawa in which the city is seen as an instrument of knowledge: a landscape that educates and transforms man's sensitivity and consequently modifies his way of seeing. Man sees the world in terms of the constant renovation he perceives when receptive to the transformations taking place around him. These transformations change and re-orient his sensitivity; man, however, is not a passive spectator, since he creates objects which are then inserted into the urban landscape and become part of what is produced in this very landscape. Hayakawa says that in this way we are enclosed in an endless circle of expression, a constant exchange between the world and our sensitivity, and our sensitivity and the world, which forms a loop, a fold. During this never-ending process our gaze is ceaselessly restructured.

Furthermore, this case is a highly unusual one in that the city in question is Tokyo, an extraordinarily overpopulated urban conglomeration lacking any apparent order. A city characterized by excess and eclecticism; a heterogeneous jumble with objects and meanings superimposed on each other, obeying no hierarchy, where nothing is stable, everything repeats itself, expands, endures and continues. Tokyo is the quintessence of congestion. →

The passage which links the bedrooms with the living room of House B seen from the garden.

Ground floor.

View from the street.

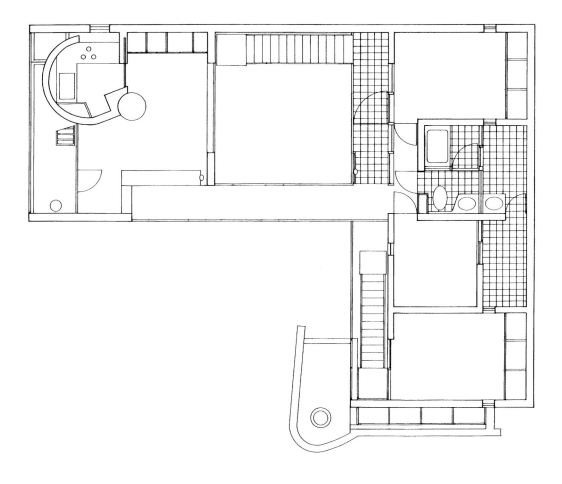

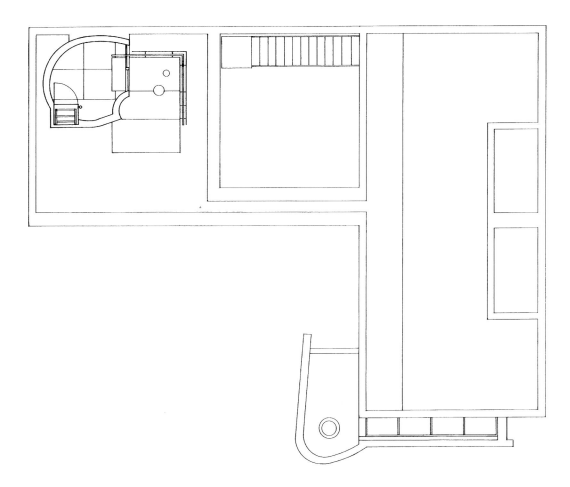

Rather than something against nature, however, the city might be understood as a natural environment; then its works of architecture would behave as organisms subject to a necessary evolution. This might sound like entelechy, granted, but things can be no other way. The buildings that survive are those whose internal laws foster better adaptation to the environment, in this case changing city conditions. Form is thus related to the need for survival.

Architects contribute to the city by transmitting new messages, but architecture can also guide each observer toward greater awareness in the midst of the confusion of signs that populate the city. For Hayakawa, architecture has the ability to make certain distinctive qualities of cities more evident by presenting them as deformed or simply filtered by sensitivity. In many cases this transformation is achieved through color, by means of which forms are often broken down into different elements. Hayakawa claims that his is a plural architecture, in which many motifs of equal value appear and disappear on the surface of a building. Color is not used to make harmonious compositions; at times, it seems to be simply the property of some volume or other. In the Sakuragoaka house, blue belongs to the cylinder which is an appliance container. It is a deep, intense blue that endows the element with an unusual presence when seen both from inside and outside. The house was conceived for two different generations: House A for the parents, and House B for the son and his family. The main living room and adjacent bedroom in House A are separated by translucent partitions which can be opened when necessary. On the other hand, the main room and bedroom in House B are separated by a bridge, two spatial compositions that contrast with each other.

The exterior walls are of smooth bare concrete, around 30% of which consists of glazed surfaces, a percentage somewhat higher than normal in private houses. The idea was to create a spatial continuity between interior and exterior and for the house to remain open to its surroundings.

Some elements that may well be called appliances are included in the project; they are mainly developed around the blue cylinder in the main room of House B. The cylinder is itself an

Second floor

Third floor.

View of House A from the garden.

View from the interior across the patio toward the south.

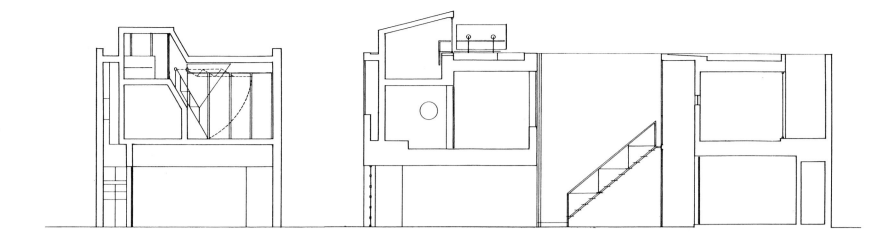

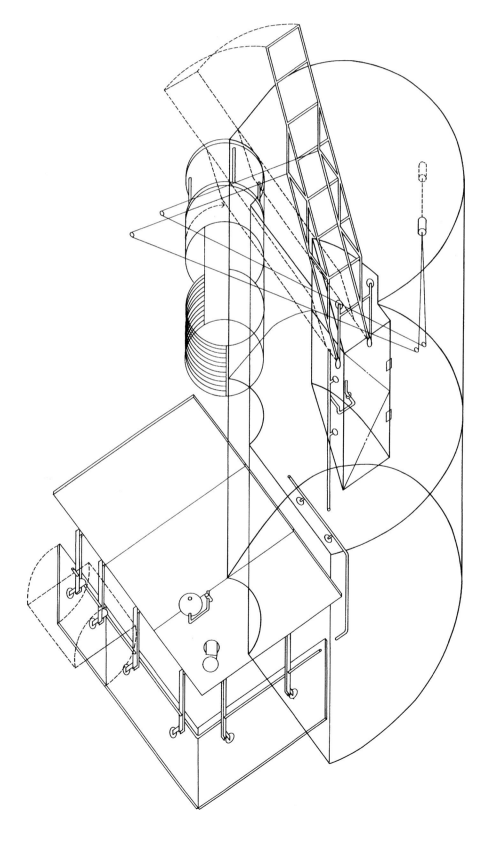

appliance containing the kitchen on the third floor and the tatami room on the fourth. Another cylinder that intersects with this contains the air conditioning as well as other necessary leisure appliances, such as the television and other audio-visual complements. In short, it is an integrated appliance that emits air, sound and images.

Inside the cylinder there is also a folding ladder which leads to the tatami room on the fourth floor. This room, with a ceiling that rises from 5 to 6 feet, has no specific function; it is a tiny attic, secluded from everyday life, which might be described as a contemporary tea room or even a folie inside the house. Next to this room there is a terrace that provides water and light. The handrail consists of half-inch-thick aluminum panels, one of which has been broken to leave room for a table.

Sections.

Axonometric. Main room in House A

Main room in House B.

The tatami room inside the blue cylinder.

Margarida House

Color helps to underline the contrast between elements
and finishes, great emphasis
having been placed on the quality of each of the elements.

Aranda, Pigem, Vilalta architects

Rafael Aranda (Olot, 1961), Carme Pigem (Olot 1962), and Ramon Vilalta (Vic, 1960) all graduated in architecture from the Escuela Técnica Superior de Arquitectura del Vallés (ETSAV), Barcelona, in 1987. Vilalta studied for a doctorate and Master's Degree in Landscape Architecture. Both Vilalta and Pigem are now teachers at the Projects Workshop at the same school where they previously studied. The team has been awarded several prizes, notably: Lighthouse in Punta Aldea, Las Palmas de Gran Canaria, MOPU (1st prize), Hotel ****Albons, Girona, Houses for the Olympic Village, Banyoles, Barcelona'92, and the Saikaibashi restaurant and shopping mall in Nagasaki, Japan.

Casa Margarida, in the town of Olot, is a single-family house designed to be used as a main residence.

The project derives from the peculiarities of the site and the suggestions proposed by the surroundings. Two essential aspects characterize the site: firstly, the orientation, which is favorable on the street side and, secondly, the steep slope of this same street.

A white volume rises from behind the gray wall which borders the plot. It has a large opening protected by white, slatted blinds which simply, cleanly and purely tone the light. This two-story block accommodates most of the spaces of the house. Another lower volume, grey in color like the wall onto the street, is placed inside it. This second volume contains the kitchen and, on the level below, the garage. The project includes only two further elements: a canopy producing a horizontal line of shade, which divides the large opening of the main volume in two, and the chimneys, which provide contrast.

It is an architecture of simple, strict volumes, which draws on a limited repertoire of shapes, elements and materials; a composition in which simplicity predominates, where the articulation of the different parts creates spatial richness. The encounter between the constructive elements is skilfully resolved and the structural forms are clear. →

View from the street.

View from the garden.

The encounter between the two volumes and the canopy.

Detail of the canopy.

View from the swimming pool area.

This page:

Plan of the garages, the garden floor and the upper floor.

Color and materials contribute to underline the architectural dialog, the different finishes permitting the identification and differentiation of each element so that the whole is enriched by the nuances and variations of each of its parts.

The white body withdraws from the street and is isolated to ensure greater privacy. Its appearance is one of lightness, in contrast with the darker, heavier kitchen volume, which is inserted into it and protects it as a continuation of the base.

The garden and the swimming pool are on the same plane with respect to the house and street level, at the highest point of the site. The entrance, on the other hand, is sited on the lowest part of the plot, adjoining the street. In this way, access is not through the garden but through a patio at garage level and some stairs which climb up to the second floor. Thus, the swimming pool and the garden do not form a semi-public space, as is usually the case, but stand in a completely isolated area thanks to the existence of the public patio.

Entry is produced neither brusquely nor immedi-ately: the approach is gradual and initial contact with the house is only partial. Comprehension of the house is a progressive process, as the visitor follows the itinerary from one space to the next. The core is a double-height space over the dining room. The different spaces are arranged around this void and are characterised by the varying presence of natural light and by the visual play of reflections and transparencies. On one side, the living room. On the floor above, a balcony connects the stair with the study.

The interior spaces echo the patterns of the slats; the shadow play is enhanced by the different positions. Whether open or closed, the blinds skilfully protect the large glazed surface from direct sunlight. Since both facades are open, it is possible to see right through the building.

Permanent qualities of the project are concern for the lighting and the superimposition of different skins that filter the light and establish a subtle relationship between interior and exterior. The study of light led the architects to design complex elements, such as the canopy which runs →

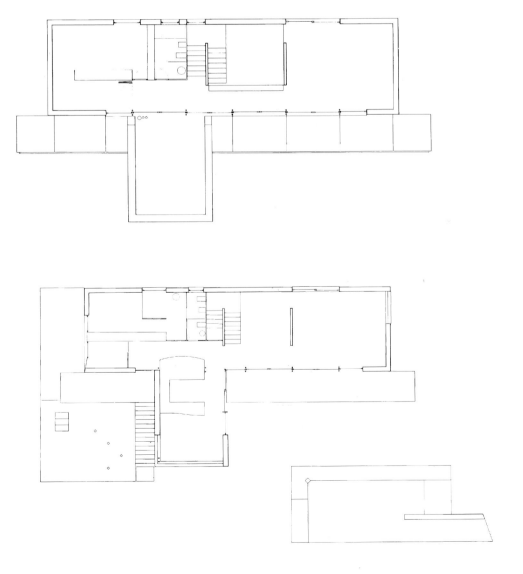

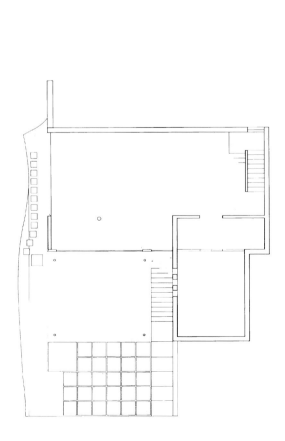

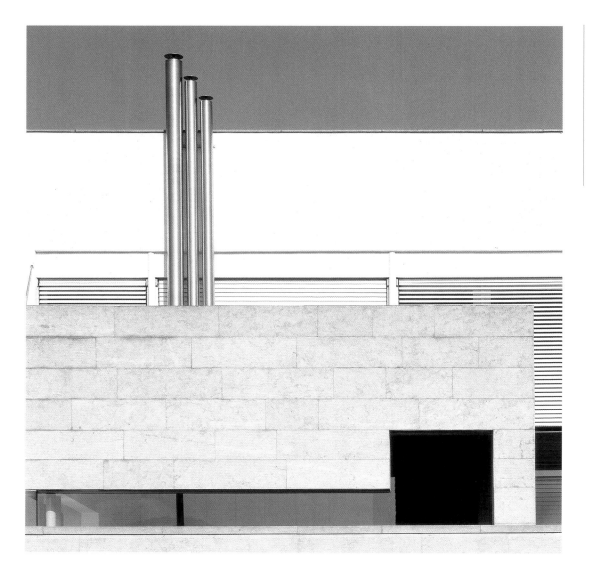

Part of the facade seen from the street.

View of the living room from the kitchen.

Section and ground plans of the dwelling and swimming-pool section.

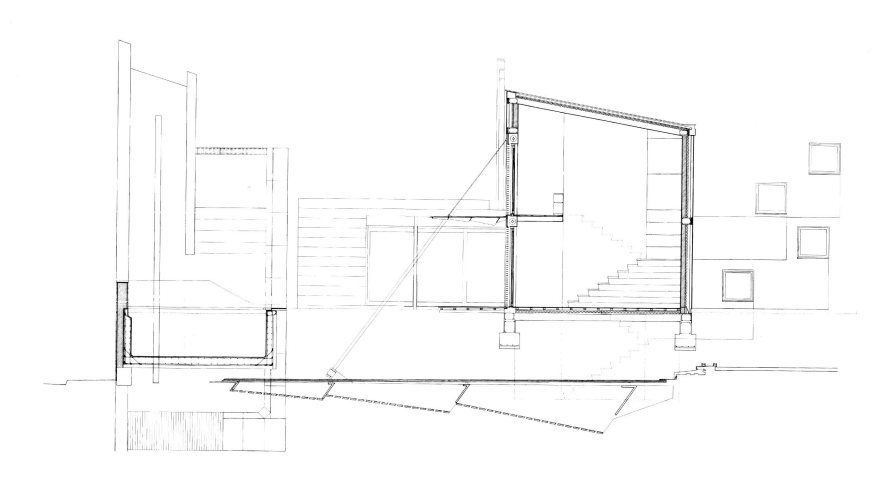

The living room.

View from the study.

View from the living room.

the length of the garden facade of the white volume, interrupted only where it meets the volume below. The lower part consists of slats of bolondo wood, forming three planes whose slopes differ slightly from each other. The first skin of translucent glass filters the light; the second, made of fillets, produces striped shadows.

Both in its volumetric solution and small scale, the project is remarkable for its economy of resources. For example, the horizontal steel profile acts as both a girder to support the balcony over the double space and the box for the roll-up blind, while the handrail includes a low piece of furniture. Every detail is treated in the simplest possible manner.

Nonetheless, efforts to employ the minimum number of necessary elements are accompanied by the search for subtleness and complexity, which induced the architects to play with textures, with the qualities of wood, to open small apertures which upgrade the intermediate spaces and to neatly resolve some of the →

The bedroom entry.

Detail of the bathroom.

The double space seen
from the stair.

spaces which are often assigned lesser importance in projects, such as the bathroom, the kitchen or the corridors.

The large glazed surface completely opens the house to the garden and the surrounding views, while the other openings are precise cut-outs which frame the lawn, a tree or some other specific detail. The architects were as careful in their treatment of the image of the building as in the construction of the exterior as a visual prolongation of the interior spaces.

Can Cardenal

The initial project consisted of the construction
of a small guest pavilion
as an extension to the masia Can Cardenal in Batet de la Serra (Olot).

**Aranda, Pigem,
Vilalta architects**

"It approaches but doesn't harm the *masia*,
It resembles but doesn't copy the masia,
It moves away from but doesn't forget the masia".

These rather enigmatic lines refer to the guest house at the Girona masia (manor-farmhouse) of Can Cardenal and the words, paradoxical yet exact, were written by the three Catalan architects who designed it. Opposition, difference, and paradox: the project is held together by the most fragile of threads.

Stone and granite, the former rough and the latter smooth, opaque and transparent, old and new. Before and now. Maybe one against the other, but above all one with and for the other, the meeting of opposites. A harmonious confrontation that creates a fascinating dialog of contrasts whose points of encounter and complete meaning are revealed precisely in contradiction. The initial project consisted of a small guest pavilion annexed to the main Can Cardenal dwelling in Batet de la Serra (Olot).

The architects were faced with this rural dwelling characteristic of inland Catalonia, consisting of →

Ground plan of the whole complex.

General view of the location of the Can Cardenal masia in Batet de la Serra (Olot).

The pavilion produces a disturbing sensation of unreality, strengthened by the reflections of the trees on the polished surfaces.

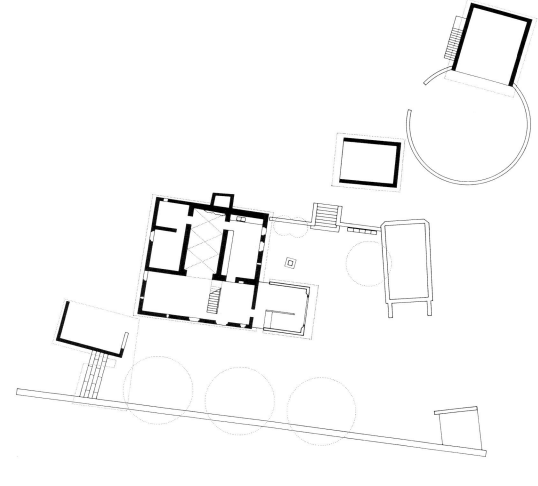

the family home and a series of outbuildings, standing alone in a vast agricultural setting. Thick stone walls, large dimensions, added rooms, austerity, opaqueness ... . An unwonted beauty, the result neither of careful composition nor of skilful design; a primary beauty born of traditional construction techniques, immediate forms whose massive walls conceal the memory of time.

"A masia has no more value than the years of its history; it suggests that the new architectural piece, like the different phases which have made up the whole, denotes the moment of intervention", state the architects. A value they hint at by adding distance with their pavilion.

This conception holds one of the keys in the search for opposites in order to at last create a dialog between architectures, a conversation through time.

The square two-story pavilion attached to the east facade of the masia further extends the latter's south-facing facade in this direction. The point where the two constructions meet is a vertical strip of translucent glass that acts as a visual separating element.

The material used and its treatment endow the pavilion walls with a disturbing sensation of unreality and magic. Polished green granite blocks form a continuous, compact body, creating at the same time a surprising impression of transparency. The smooth, shining texture of the walls, where the reflections of the trees create ethereal images, produces a sharp contrast with the roughness of the old stone walls. →

Stone and granite, rough and smooth, opaque and transparent, old and new. The contrast between the two constructions creates a harmonious meeting of opposites.

Detail of the glass strip which acts as a visual separation element between the two constructions.

A section of the east facade, where the two levels can be appreciated, the upper (a balcony) and the lower (a bedroom).

The pavilion walls are constructed of thick polished granite blocks, at once massive and fragile.

The unreal, magical sensation of the pavilion is once again reinforced by the chosen solution for the roof. This flat slab of concrete, massive yet fragile, rests on practically imperceptible steel pillars so that it appears to float above the walls. To a certain extent, the east facade of the pavilion breaks up the continuity and heterogeneity of the construction. On this facade square granite blocks joined together by an also imperceptible steel lattice form an original gridiron. The granite blocks appear to be suspended in mid-air, again creating an unreal yet markedly geometric image. Even so, this panel of plaques does have an additional function, that of revealing the true thickness of the material and its function as wall covering.

Similarly, the east facade does not stretch the full height of the building, the upper part remaining as an open space, like a balcony. A balcony is precisely what the second floor of the pavilion is: a space open to the wide views, the vast uninhabited territory which surrounds the site.

The nighttime image of this interplay between open and closed spaces, between wall and air, is fascinating to say the least. The lower part of the facade corresponds to the bedroom. The light on the first floor pierces the walls through the honeycombs which separate the granite plaques. The exterior image is that of an enormous shining gridiron suspended in darkness.

The guest house is characterized by simple, friendly forms. The play of light and shadow is conveyed inside, where it is the sun that casts the shadow of the gridiron onto the guests' beds.

Light and shadow. A new meeting of opposites added to the harmonious contrast of stone and granite, rough and smooth, opacity and trans-→

The pavilion's east facade consists of square, granite plaques, separated in a strictly geometric way, and an open terrace above.

The nighttime image of the pavilion's east facade is at least fascinating. The lower light is that of the guest bedroom.

The pavilion roof, supported on steel pillars, seems to levitate above the building.

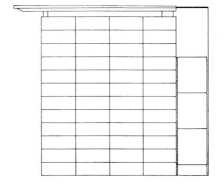 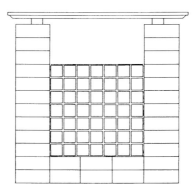 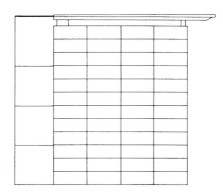

Elevations of the three facades
which make up the pavilion.
The east facade (in the centre)
breaks up the construction's
homogeneity.

Detail of the solution used for
the roof in which the almost
imperceptible steel support pillars can be seen.

The pavilion's top floor is a terrace open to the panoramic
views of the vast territory
which surrounds the masia.

Detail of the east facade, where the steel lattice joins the plaques.

Interior view of the top floor.

The guest bedroom is on the first floor. The play of light created by the east facade is continued inside.

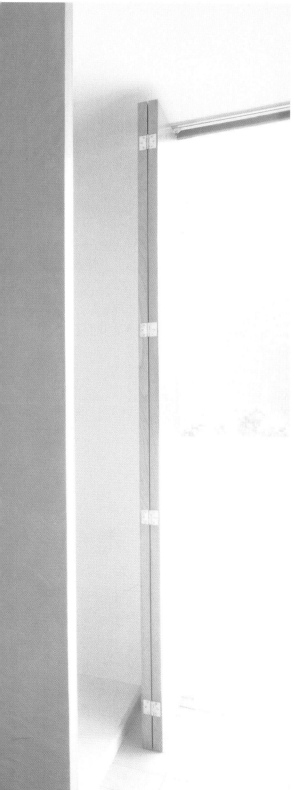

parency, old and new, solid and ethereal. Before and now. "Both in concept and in form, both in construction and in materials. Large hollows and small hollows, green and black, length and width. The walls are not burdened, wood does not exist, the cut piece prevails".

The forms manage to transmit the ideas that originated them. A close proximity exists between what the architects set out to express and what they actually do express. Paradox provides the effective backbone for the project's inner coherence. The masia reveals the impor-

tance and meaning of its particular history and its new neighbour approaches it without harming it, resembling it without copying it, and moving away without forgetting it.

Dub House

Not only grand gestures
but also small details
can potentially enrich our daily lives.

Architecturbüro Bolles-Wilson

The married couple formed by Peter Wilson (Melbourne, 1950) and Julia Bolles (Münster, 1948), created their own studio in London in 1980 and later in the German town of Münster. First as a student and later as a teacher, Peter Wilson was one of the leading figures of the most fruitful years of the Architectural Association of London. His first works, like the Münster Library, the Blackburn House in London and the Suzuki House in Tokyo, have become points of reference in present-day architecture.

"Not only grand gestures but also small details can potentially enrich our daily lives". The architecture of Bolles-Wilson can be read in many ways. It has an immediate reading, which the color harmony, the combination of materials and diverse geometries is capable of immediately transmitting to any spectator who contemplates their buildings. And a second reading, the legacy of the Architectural Association, the innovating and lucid look at the complexity of contemporary urban society, the overlapping of spaces, differ-

ent scales and information networks. A reflection which relates to other architects of the same school, like Elia Zenghelis, Rem Koolhaas, Bernard Tschumi or Zaha Hadid, who burst with unprecedented force onto the architectural scene in the mid eighties. A third reading is related to the Wilsons' contact with Japanese culture, which led to their combining the concern for complexity mentioned above with a growing search for simplicity, an effort to empty objects of superimposed identities or immediate refer-

Overall sketch of the house: the atrium, in its original state in the drawing above and with Wilson's addition in the one below.

The final result of the "adjustment", to use Wilson's term, carried out in this modern-style house from the sixties. Simple forms and the vertical/horizontal interplay characterize the project.

The shining blue of the small-tile wall strongly enhances the architectural whole. The new wall breaks up the original uniform height, the "artificial horizon".

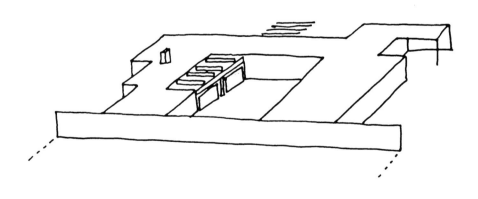

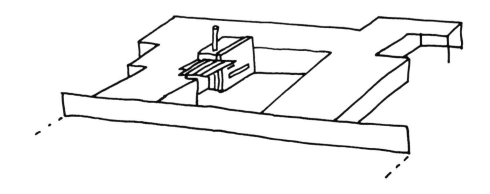

General plan of the project, red underlining in the interior patio of a modern house-atrium from the sixties. The continuous red line corresponds to the blue wall and the broken line to the zinc study.

The contrast between the two new walls is at once marked and harmonious. The photograph also shows the system chosen for the roof.

ences, leaving them free to express themselves; thus one reading after another, all superimposed. They therefore display the surprising and laudable ability to produce buildings far removed from theoretical discourse in which theory is not revealed in any loud or pamphleteering way, which is what normally characterizes works by those who set out to state their convictions in an excessively forthright manner. Their method of translating architectural ideas to projects is informed by an attitude that lies somewhere in-between the intuitive and the pragmatic and endows their buildings with solidity. "The origins of architecture are to be found in the world of ideas and its validity in the kingdom of utility", Wilson himself declares.

The project for the Dub House involves alterations (minor corrections) to a modern-style house from the sixties. The plans reveal that although the intervention affects only a small sector of the house, it has major repercussions on its image. Upon this basis, and in a dialectical way, Bolles and Wilson began to introduce interplays of planes, horizontal and vertical displacements. The first "addition", to use their own term, consists of a deep blue ceramic gresite wall in the interior patio: a forthright, optimistic explosion of color. An element of greater height which breaks with the "artificial horizon line drawn by the existing roof", in the words of Wilson, and taking advantage of this difference in height to permit the creation of a lengthwise interior skylight.

The second added element is a study contiguous with the blue wall, slightly lower, clad with zinc outside and wood inside. This second wall features a set of windows of different sizes, at dif- →

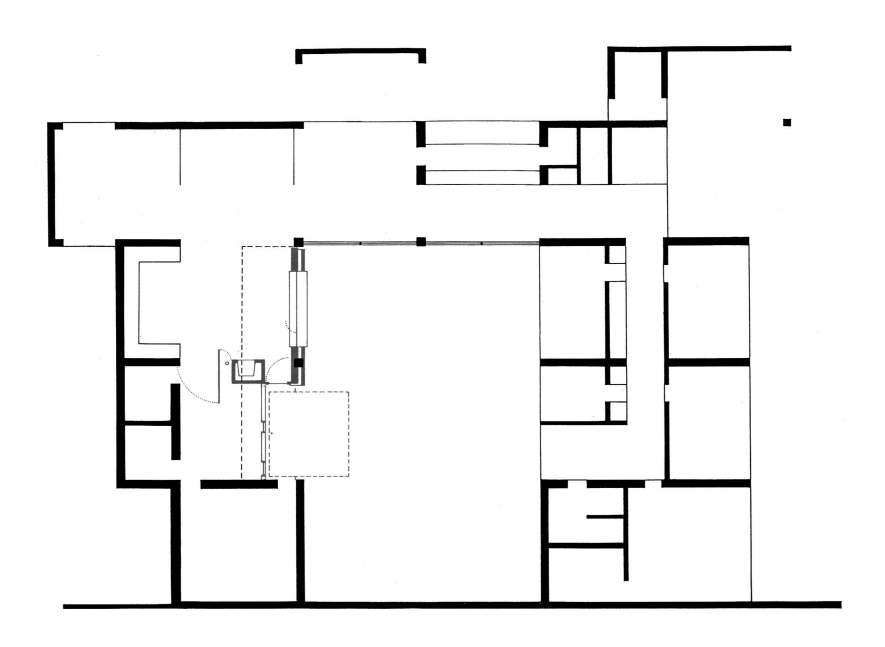

ferent heights, and reminiscent of Neoplasticism. The third addition, unlike the two earlier ones, is a horizontal plane: a pergola of zinc bars that occupies the space created by the slight displacement between the two earlier-mentioned walls, between which an entry has been built.

There are two more elements inside: a geometric fireplace with a circular aluminum smoke-extraction shaft and a large revolving wooden door, almost a swinging wall.

Five elements: two walls, a pergola, a fireplace and a door. Elements as simple and forthright as words. The result: a short phrase introduced into a old text, or perhaps the short last line of a Japanese haiku that turns the whole poem upside down.

The interiors are also characterized by simple forms. The photograph shows the inside of the structure faced with blue brick, the lounge, of a powerful pure white, together with two new elements: the fireplace and the revolving wall.

Elevations of the project, in which we can see the two new walls, of different heights, and the pergola.

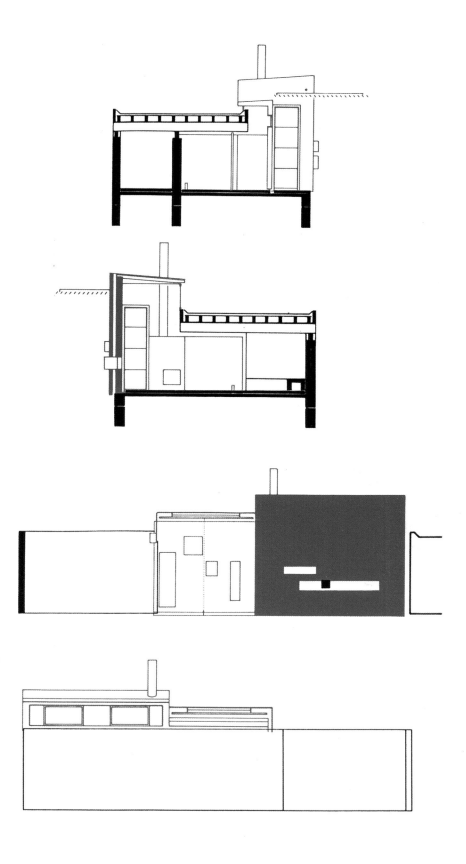

The zinc wall hides a timber study, also characterized by simple forms and the lack of ornamentation. The strict geometry is repeated in the interiors.

Following page:

The chosen form for the fireplace is a paradigm of this simplicity, fruit of Wilson's admiration for the clarity of Functionalism. The fireplace is reduced to its minimum structure without sacrificing either beauty or utility.

Lawson-Westen House

The formal language employed both in the interiors
and the façades obey the application of
very concrete ideas about domestic matters

Eric Owen Moss

The career of the Californian architect, Eric Owen Moss, from its beginnings in the early sixties, has been characterised by the volition to break with the postulates of rationalism and the rigidity of pre-defined schemes which do not allow experimentation nor pure invention. His first works were centred on the dwelling theme, works such as the Triplex Apartments (King's Beach, 1974 - 1976), the Morgensten Warehouse (Los Angeles 1977 - 1979), the Petal House (West Los Angeles, 1982 - 1984), or the projects of the Fun House (Hidden Valley, 1980) and the Pin Ball House (Los Angeles, 1980 - 1984) which were far ahead of the established order, in a continuous spatial and structural exploration. On a larger scale one must mention his projects of office or service blocks, like those of the World Savings and Loan (Los Angeles, 1983 - 1985) 8522 National Boulevard (Culver City, 1986 - 1090), Central Housing Office Building, University of California, (Irvine, 1986 - 1989) or the Paramount Laundry Building (Culver City, 1987 - 1089).

On the contrary to what a first impression might produce, the Lawson - Westen House does not constitute a mere formal "tour de force" or a visual and scenographic display based on arbitrary whims, the clients own functional, spatial and in some cases formal ideas were collected and interpreted by the architect, forming the true premises for the project, so that the spatial and formal experimentation constituted the architectonic translation of previously-existing ideas.

The special organisation of the house converts the kitchen into the true centre, both functional and spatial, emphasised by the conical roof→

The façade, in coloured stucco, which gives onto the garden. In the foreground are the laminated wood beams that support the rectangular-bodied dome and which emerge incomplete on the exterior.

In the garden access of the south façade, the special combination of window elements creates a double-height abstract composition.

The façade which gives
onto the rear garden with
the access stairs direct to
the first floor. The conical
roof is adapted according
to the necessities of each
interior space.

also the main component of the building's composition, by virtue not only of its size but also of its function as generator of other forms which make up the exterior image.

The formal language employed both in the interiors and the facades obeys the application of very specific ideas about domestic matters, with ground-breaking results that nevertheless reflect concern for detail and for total design, in a conceptual dissection of the house on all its levels. Owen Moss did not restrict himself to a harmonious ordering of a series of conventional spaces; he conceives architecture as a method of exploring all the possibilities that a given space may generate.

Throughout his work, Eric Owen Moss' mastery of the use and combination of materials, especially wood (Philip Johnson once described him as a "jeweller of wood"), is revealed in the careful design of every constituent part of his projects, from major structural elements to the smallest piece of furniture.

The Lawson-Westen House stands in one of Los Angeles' wealthiest suburbs on a rectangular site perpendicular to the street, very common in this part of town, which largely determined the →

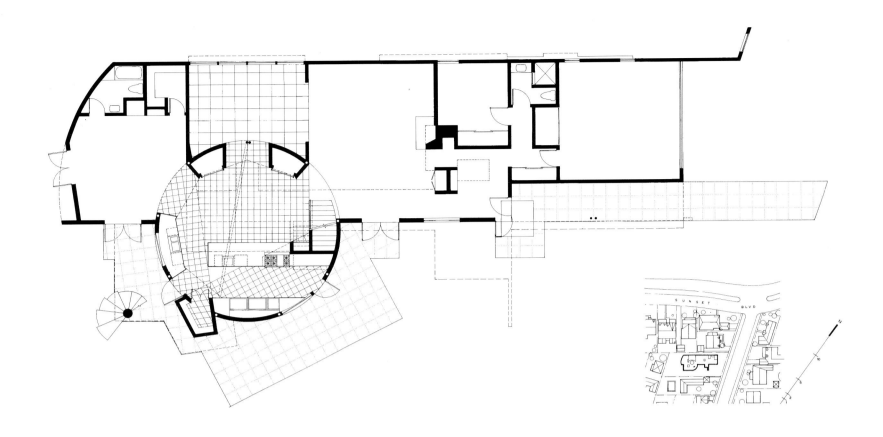

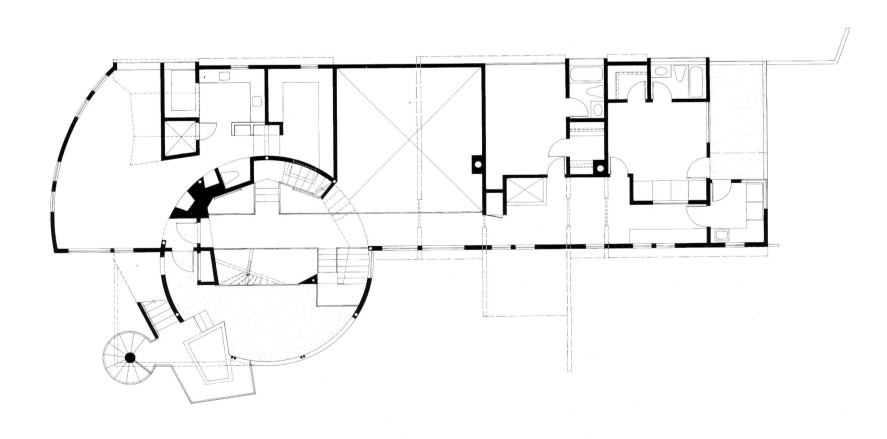

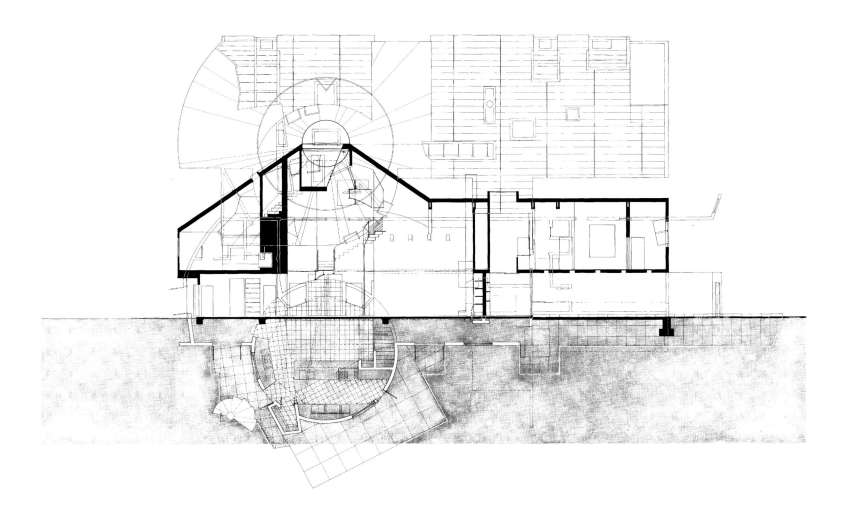

The ground floor.

The first floor.

A longitudinal section through the
body of the cone.

Sketch.

The access facade to the dwelling, the only one in bare concrete. On the second floor, the distorted corner window above the laundry room.

The spatial communication between the kitchen, living room and dining room forms a large communal area which was one of the owners' initial requirements.

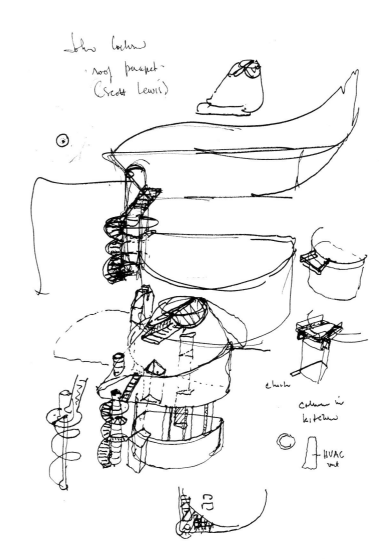

shape of the house. Its position along the northern edge of the plot made it possible to place a garden in front of the south facade, thus creating a more intense interior/exterior relationship, one of the initial requirements on the part of the clients.

The access, both for vehicles and pedestrians, is at one end of the building, while inside a→

Axonometric of the roof from the interior.

Axonometric of the conical volume over the kitchen.

The living room beneath the vaulted body, crossed by a passageway on the second floor which links both sections of the house and communicates spatially and visually with the kitchen and dining room.

sequential itinerary is followed that ends in the kitchen, the true functional and spatial nucleus of the dwelling.

The owners had decided that the program should develop around the kitchen. The ground floor contains the communal areas linked together; the kitchen, equipped almost for professionals, has a perimeter ring where the service and storage areas are concentrated and where the main stair begins. The large living room is covered by a dome of considerable height (another idea from the owners), in which a metal-

lic chimney soars up in sculptural fashion. Contiguous to both, the dining room is on a more domestic scale. This floor is completed with a games room, adjacent to the kitchen on the west facade, and the garage and the guest area in the eastern zone.

The central position of the stair produces on the second floor a layout divided into two opposite zones, linked by a passageway over the living room. The west zone, with the master bedroom and its dependencies, has direct access to an outside terrace with jacuzzi, and communi- →

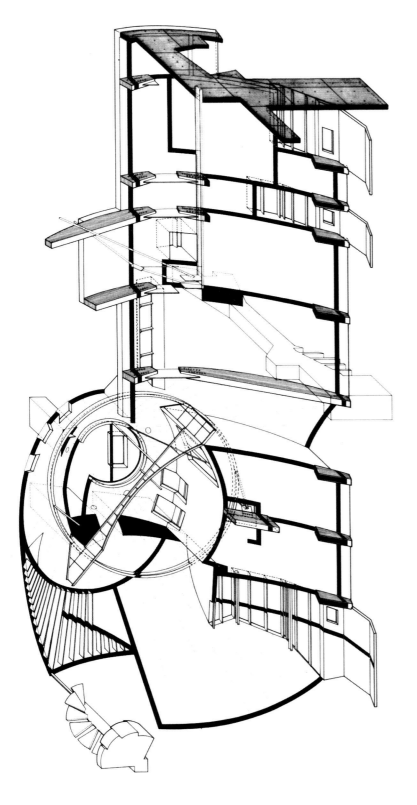

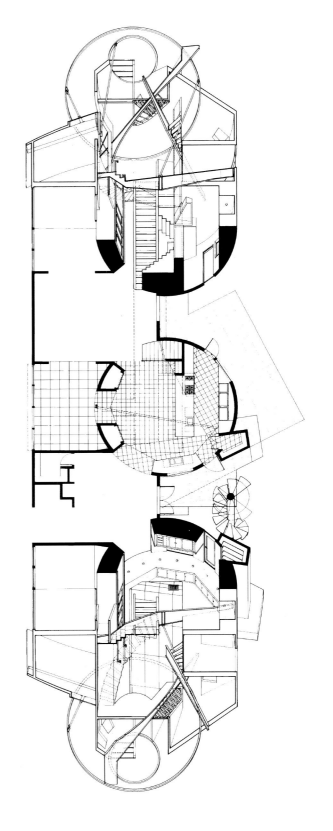

cates with the garden by way of an exterior spiral stair. The eastern zone accommodates two bedrooms and the laundry room, above which a distorted corner window characterizes the access facade. In the empty space above the kitchen the stair marks the perimeter as it climbs in continuous circles and surprising visual changes toward a small ocean observatory on top of the conical roof.

The building is a dissection and posterior recomposition of its constituent parts, all of which play a major role in the definition of the dwelling. For example, Moss agrees with the idea that the skylights (an element suggested by the clients) determine the profile of the conical roof.

The inclusion of structural elements in the definition of spaces is another of the characteristics of the house. Circular metal beams, which appear in the living room later to disappear and then reappear outside, constitute together with an intermediate wood frame the structure of the conical roof. The empty interior space below is crisscrossed with almost diametrical metal girders that support the different platforms and stairs

and contribute to the hotch-potch of forms and materials that characterize the volume above the kitchen. The laminated timber beams which generate the vault of the rectangular body appear dramatically on the south facade as incomplete elements of what might have been the roof.

The use and combination of different materials such as wood, glass and metal carry with them a special attention to details in the design of elements such as the access door to the grounds, the fireplace in the living room, the wood profiles in the vaulted roof or the wide repertoire of windows. Each one of these elements contributes individually and collectively to the definition of the dwelling.

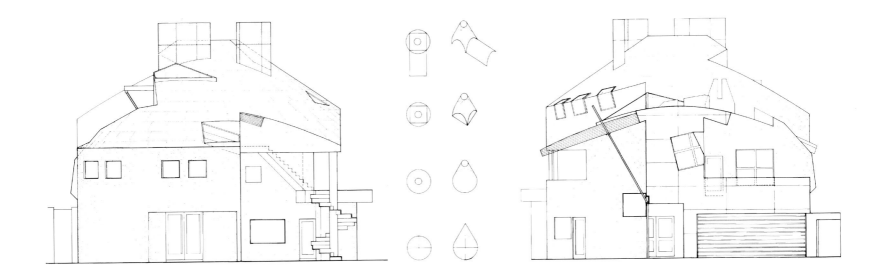

6/20/89

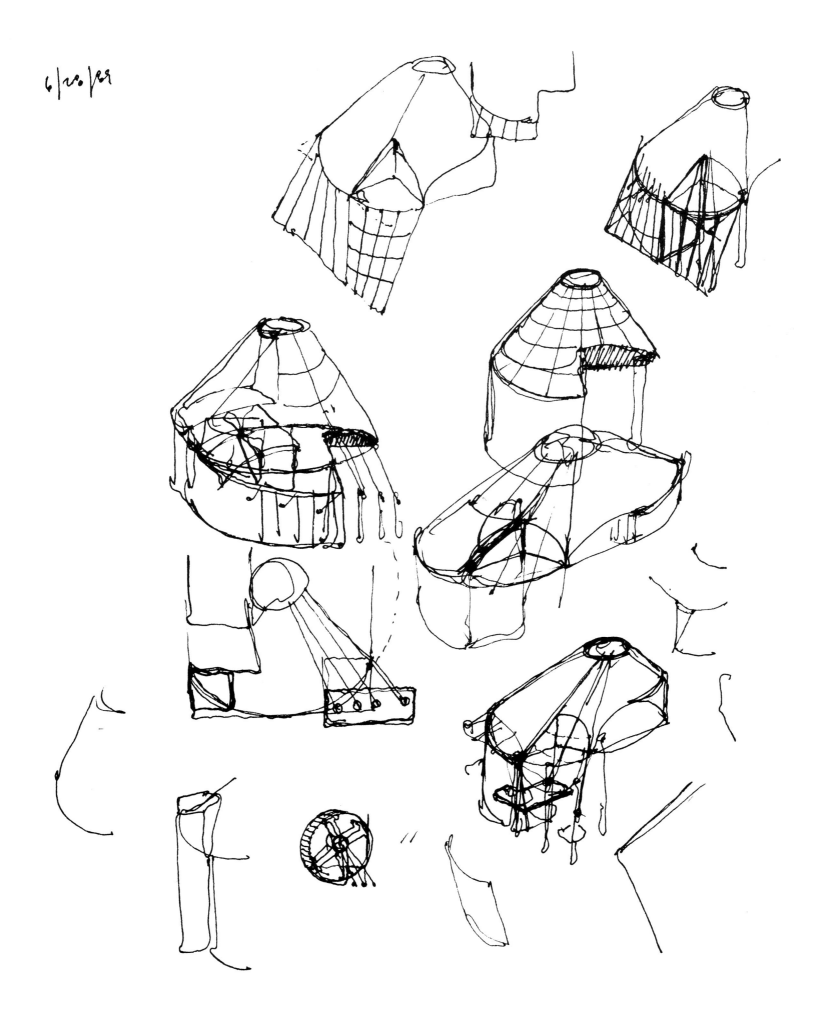

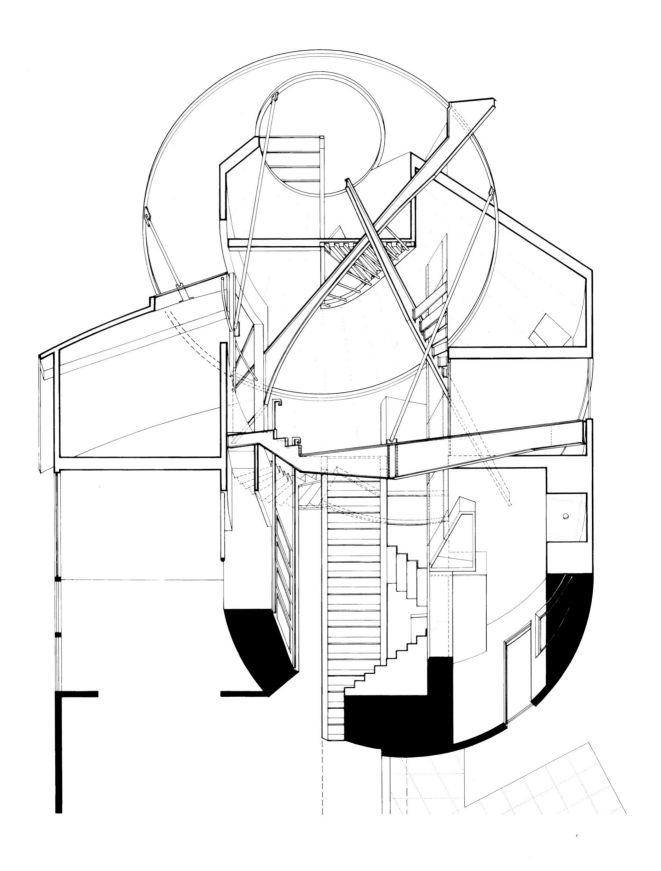